Affective Subjects
in the Classroom
EXPLORING RACE, SEX, AND DRUGS

Affective Subjects in the Classroom

EXPLORING RACE, SEX, AND DRUGS

Charlotte Epstein
Temple University

Intext Educational Publishers
College Division of Intext
Scranton • San Francisco • Toronto • London

ISBN 0-7002-2416-5

Copyright ©, 1972, International Textbook Company

Library of Congress Catalog Card Number: 74-185818

For Paulette,
    who persistently resisted the
    effects of bad education

and for Grace and Alvin,
    who supported her

Acknowledgment

These strategies were refined in the crucible of the Teacher Corps Program at Temple University. Ms. Elaine Blake, Lecturer in Curriculum and Instruction, and Dr. Evan Sorber, now Associate Curriculum and Instruction Chairman for Early Childhood and Elementary Education, provided much of the heat for that crucible. They brought some of the strategies from their own experiences and let me adapt them, they made creative suggestions for changing some of the other strategies, and tested still others with students. Above all, they provided an atmosphere of fun and excitement and success that encouraged me to continue to work on the techniques and to inspire other teachers to use them. My thanks!

Contents

*Affective Subjects
in the Classroom*
EXPLORING RACE, SEX, AND DRUGS

Introduction

This book has a number of purposes that arise logically from certain philosophical commitments.

Commitment Number One: In the education of teachers for the practice of their profession, it is necessary to teach them in the way that they should teach children. That is, the strategies and methods that are useful in the teaching of children are also useful in the teaching of teachers. Not only are they useful in teacher education, they are vital; for almost inevitably the teacher will teach in the ways she was taught. Especially when she is faced with a crisis in the classroom—a crisis in discipline, perhaps, or in learning—whatever she has read or heard about methods is forgotten, and she falls back on the methods that were used on her. There is no substitute in teacher education for actually experiencing the methods that must be used with children.

The purpose of this book, then, is to describe methods for use in the education of teachers. The difference between using the methods with children and using them in teacher education is that, after using a technique with teachers, it is necessary for teachers to step out of the role of students and analyze the technique just used.

They identify the various steps, examine the rationale for each and then go on to practice using the technique so that they develop the necessary skills.

First, they should use the technique on each other, exchanging helpful criticism. When they feel somewhat confident in the use of the method, then they may try it with children, and bring back to their colleagues reports of how it worked and how they felt in using it. In discussing their experiences, they can determine what errors they made and how they may use whatever unexpected responses they got from the children.

Commitment Number Two: Every subject must be explored not only on the cognitive level but also on the affective level. Often, we struggle and fail in our attempts to help children "achieve" in school because we are ignoring their strong feelings that must be dealt with before they can cope with "facts." There is no subject that can be taught legitimately without concern for the learner's feelings. Thus, feelings about self need to be part of the classroom material before mathematics becomes important for some children, feelings about adults need to be explored before information about drugs can be internalized, and feelings about race need to be expressed before history and civics take on any real meaning.

Both majority and minority youngsters are caught up today in the feelings generated by changing relationships between groups. Young Indian people, young Black people, young Chicanos, Chinese-Americans, Japanese-Americans are all in the vanguard of movements for self-determination, and assertion of self and group identity. Young Caucasians have their own struggle for identity, partly in the reflection of minority movements and partly in their relations with adults. And poor youngsters of all racial and nationality groups are actively resisting the assaults on their egos caused by poverty and exclusion. For all of these young people there is a tremendous investment of emotion as they fight for lives as complete human beings. Their feelings as they struggle are facts of monumental importance.

Another purpose of this book, then, is to provide ways in which the teacher and her pupils may begin to make feelings as respectable a concern in the classroom as facts have always been.

Commitment Number Three: Adults, including teachers, must admit that they do not have the answers to most serious human problems. The past fifty years have produced fantastic changes, which have created and exacerbated the problems of interaction and survival. Obviously, we must find solutions to these problems—drug addiction, interracial conflict, destructive relationships between the sexes, and ineffective political functioning, among others. If we limit our teaching function to the defining of problems as we see them and reviewing only the solutions that have already been tried, we are retarding the emergence of new definitions and new solutions.

This book suggests strongly that teachers recognize their own limitations in knowledge and problem solving and adopt teaching strategies that will make them feel so active and excited and successful that the recognition of those limitations will represent no ego threat.

Commitment Number Four: We can educate the next generation to solve many of our problems if we are courageous enough to free them from our own prejudices and anxieties. There are many teachers who have the courage but simply do not know what steps to take to help the children go off in new directions. Nor are they equipped to deal with colleagues and administrators who resist this way of working with children.

The methods described in this book are designed to free the children to express feelings, raise questions, define problems and test solutions that will make a difference in their own lives and in future generations. They are also useful in helping teachers develop skill in dealing with other adults in their professional lives.

Commitment Number Five: A significant number of teachers and prospective teachers at all levels of education are brave, caring, and skillful. This book offers support and additional assistance to them.

1

The Problem Census

Description of the Technique

Teacher (to the class): What would you like to know about race?

She immediately writes the question on the board, then turns back to the class and says again, "What would you like to know about race?"* Then she waits. After the question is asked and there is some silence, the students begin to respond. (If there is a very long silence, the teacher reads the question aloud just as she has written it.) As the students respond, the teacher writes each response verbatim on the board. She makes no comment. She is merely the recorder for the students' responses. Occasionally, the teacher asks a student if she has written his response correctly. Or she may ask a student to help her get his response down exactly.

After six or seven responses have been recorded, there is silence. The teacher says nothing. She merely waits, looking at the students,

---

*The word race here refers to the idea of race as the students perceive it rather than any accurate definition of the term. The responses should indicate not only what the students say they want to know but also what they think constitutes a racial group and what they feel about different groups.

pleasantly expectant. If the silence continues beyond ten or twelve seconds, she may read the question aloud again, and then wait. The responses will probably start again. After two or three such silences, a twenty-second silence probably signifies that the census is completed.

The teacher then says, "All right. Now, I will have this whole list mimeographed for next time and give each one a copy. Then we can decide how to take up each item. Remember that this list is open-ended. Any time you want to add a question or a topic to it, feel free to do so."

The Question

The nature of the question is critical in taking a problem census. If the question does not have the necessary characteristics, the chances are that the number of responses will be small and probably of limited usefulness.

The question asked must insure that every answer is right. If we do not provide for this, then we are once more giving only certain children an opportunity to respond in class, while those who never have the "right" answer are again excluded. Whether the right answer is a fact, an opinion that agrees with the teacher's, or a conventional choice of words, we exclude from participation those pupils who have not learned the facts we think are important, those who hold opinions arising out of their own unique life experiences, and those who use words the teacher objects to because of her life experiences. Thus, a question like "What are the facts surrounding the outbreak of the Civil War?" is not a suitable question for a problem census. Though the responses will undoubtedly aid the teacher in diagnosing the level of information held by the pupils about the Civil War, she may hear nothing from pupils who have ideas and opinions that do not appear in traditional history texts. Above all, she will probably get nothing of her pupils' feelings about the Civil War and race, since the question is phrased so as to make it clear that the pupils are to give back what they have received in previous lessons.

Some teachers say that they teach about the Civil War in such a way that many historical sources are used and feelings and opinions are freely expressed and discussed. Nevertheless, there are always some students who do not absorb the body of factual material. These are the very students who probably need most desperately the opportunities for participation and recognition that a problem census affords. Also, there are students who even after the most factually complete and emotionally open lesson reject the available data because of their own emotional commitments to stereotypes and other previously learned misconceptions. These students, too, may be reluctant to jeopardize their academic standing by giving the "wrong" answer, and the teacher will never know why they are silent.

The question asked must imply that many answers are possible. Though the teacher may be thoroughly competent in the subject matter of the question, she must remember that her competency is limited by her own creativity and the creative thinking of those who have gone before her. No expert in any field has the benefit of the thinking of future generations. Consequently, we must make opportunities for young people studying today to raise questions we have not even dreamed of.

Especially in the area of race relations it is clear that the generation now working is a long way from solving the problems. Perhaps we can educate the next generation to be free from the constrictions that are making us fail. One way we can do this is by asking questions in such a way that we do not limit the responses to our notions of what they ought to be.

Thus, the question, "What has been done to solve racial problems in this country?" is not an appropriate question for a problem census. The student who can only reply "Nothing," is a rare, courageous student who is willing to risk the teacher's rejection of his answer on the grounds that it is not "correct." Most pupils will give back the information the teacher and the books have presented. Those who do not accept or cannot remember the information are excluded from the process, for they are not being asked to say what they think, or feel, or fear, or hate, or worry about. They are not being encouraged to raise questions, express doubts, or come up with brave new suggestions. For diagnostic purposes, the most that one can diagnose from such a question is the level of recall of cognitive data of those pupils who answered.

Everyone must be able to answer the question. The teacher must bear in mind that she cannot be satisfied with participation of her "bright" students, or even of a majority of the students. The goal is to get total participation. To this end, the question must be so phrased that everyone can answer. Now, it is likely that some pupils, conditioned by their school experience to being put down for wrong answers, will view with skepticism any teacher's statement assuring them that any answer is acceptable. Consequently, such assurances are superfluous. It is much more useful to ask a question that everyone *can* answer, and then to accept those answers in such a way as eventually to convince the most skeptical student.

The class must be interested in and concerned about the question. Someone may legitimately ask, "If this process really aims at students' interests and concerns how can the teacher justify making a choice of topic? Why not just ask the class, 'What do you want to study?' "

There is no doubt that there are times when students should be given absolute freedom in selecting areas of study. If we are trying to encourage curiosity, critical thinking, and creativity, then we cannot justify making all the decisions about what young people should be curious and creative about. However, the young people we teach have already been influenced by homes, schools, and social expectations. On the subject of race, for instance, they may already have learned that some races are inferior, or that race should not be discussed in mixed racial groups. From the vantage point of maturity and experience, the teacher may be aware of the problems in race relations that need solving and of the destructive effects of racism. She may also be quite sure that, though she has never heard students talk about the matter, they are prejudiced, fearful, and hostile towards other races. She knows something about adult attitudes in the community. She has observed students' behavior vis-à-vis other races. She has only to raise the question to realize that the students *are* interested and concerned. But if she does not raise the question, the chances are that no one else will.

The teacher must be interested in and concerned about the answers. There is some future implied; that is, something will be done with the answers. Pupils are not without experience of teachers who ask them what they think and what they want and yet are patently uninterested in the responses. The questions and the answers become just another classroom exercise, because the teacher has her curriculum to cover and everyone knows students don't know what's good for them.

If a teacher feels this way, she should not use the problem census technique in her classroom. Using the technique and not following through merely reinforces the lack of trust so many young people feel about their teachers. As a matter of fact, making sure to use the responses at least as part of the curriculum is an excellent way of beginning to rebuild some of that trust.

The question must be in the language of the pupils. Very often, a teacher is tempted to ask students a question using words they do not understand. This, then, presents an opportunity for the teacher to teach the meanings of the new words. Though there is certainly nothing wrong with teaching such a lesson on word usage and meaning, it should not be done in the name of the problem census. When the teacher stops to teach the meaning of the words in the question, she changes the focus of concern. She also assumes her information-giving role, which is different from her role of census-taker, and so confuses the pupils' expectations. The pupils will not know if they should respond freely and openly, or only in terms of the narrow limitations the teacher sets when she asks such questions as, "What other word has a similar meaning?"

The question should focus on a somewhat limited area. If the student responses are really to be used as the basic material for teaching and learning, then there must be some delimitation of the subject of the question. To ask students, "What do you want to know about human relationships?" will bring forth such a variety of responses, that it will be impossible to plan adequately for a series of lessons. Inevitably, some of the students would have to be told that there is no time to take up their answers. Others would be told that what they want is too broad, that they must "refine" their answers. Still others might be asked to wait until next term or another course for what they want. None of this is calculated to encourage students to respond openly to future problem census questions.

The Teacher

The teacher must not change the question if responses are not immediately forthcoming. If there is a long silence when the problem census question is first asked, the temptation is to say that the nature of the topic or the language is overwhelming the pupils. However, the teacher must resist the temptation to 1) reword the question; 2) explain the question; 3) add to the question, or 4) urge the pupils to respond, whether she does it pleasantly or impatiently. Once she starts to talk for any of these purposes, the original objective will easily be obscured. Most of us have had the experience of asking a question and not getting an immediate response and then changing the question three or four times in rapid succession until, when the responses do begin, no one is very sure which question is being answered. One of the reasons for writing the question on the board is to make sure that this is the question being answered. If the teacher finds she must repeat it (she does this only after a *long* silence), then she can read it from the board and so avoid inadvertently changing it.

The teacher must accept and record all responses. Too often, the teacher discourages student responses without realizing what she is doing. A child offers an answer to a question and the teacher may say, "Don't you think a better way to put it is . . . ?" Or she corrects the grammar, or suggests, "Don't you really mean . . . ?" It is the rare child who can muster the courage to say to a teacher, "That's what I said and that's what I mean!" The bright, self-confident pupil will be annoyed and frustrated with the constant altering of his responses, but he will probably persevere and continue to participate in class. The child who has doubts of his own ability will have those doubts reinforced. The reluctant participant will withdraw completely from answering in class. And over most of the pupils will descend the pall of cynicism that is developed by this kind of pupil-teacher interaction: One must play the school game if one wants to make it, suppress the frustration, let the teacher think her constant correcting is helpful, and not argue with authority.

Teachers may protest that what I am suggesting here is an abrogation of a basic teacher function: correcting pupils, telling them what is right, calling attention to their errors. I have no wish here to argue the educational value of this traditional teacher function. I only plead that, for the purposes and objectives of the problem census, it is advisable to relinquish this correcting role. Since the aim is to get total participation, it is better not to risk the withdrawal of those pupils who react this way to being corrected. At any rate, how pleasant it is for youngsters to have at least a short period of time in school where they can feel free to say what they want and be sure that no one will find any fault at all with their wishes or the way they express them.

The teacher must not initiate or encourage discussion of responses. The nature of the problem census process is such that students of all ages are usually quickly involved and very interested in pursuing the topic introduced. It sounds almost paradoxical to say that the teacher must not encourage discussion. Here again it sounds as if we are denying an essential teacher role. However, we do not for a moment suggest that the teacher should henceforth refrain from encouraging class discussion. The point here is that we want all pupils to have the opportunity to make responses to the problem census question. If one pupil's response is of particular interest to some of the others, or to the teacher, and the class is encouraged to discuss it immediately, then all those who have not had a chance to add their responses to the problem census will be left out. Those left out will probably be mostly those youngsters who are slow to respond for one reason or another, those who are usually overshadowed and upstaged by the quicker, brighter, more aggressive ones. And the problem census becomes merely another instrument that damages the self-concept and causes frustration.

Should a discussion start—and it often does if the right question is asked—then the teacher must promise that every response will be taken up, and she must firmly repeat the census question and continue to record the responses.

The teacher must not evaluate responses or permit others in the group to do so. As we have noted, the teacher, for this process, must accept all responses as equally valid. Not only must she refrain from evaluating a pupil's response, but she must not permit other pupils to do so. The classroom atmosphere is so permeated with the need to evaluate every pupil response, that youngsters have picked this up and feel called upon to make it known that they think a response is right or wrong every time someone says something. By identifying the rightness or wrongness of others' responses, they thereby accrue to themselves a higher evaluation. Teachers generally encourage this, and in the process play down the importance of using everyone's contributions for sharing ideas, building on others' ideas, and developing concepts cooperatively. The emphasis in the classroom, then, is on individual success, and cooperative group work is almost nonexistent. Often teachers do not realize that they are working against themselves when they try to teach pupils to work in groups and at the same time implicitly discourage them from learning to do so.

The teacher should not label the response with the respondent's name or number the responses. This seems like a minor matter, but experience has indicated that some pupils are reluctant to respond if they are forever afterwards faced with their name attached to the response. Often, especially in affective areas, a response is made impulsively, and though it may be a significant one it is immediately regretted. Perhaps it seems too revealing, perhaps it makes the student feel vulnerable in the face of prevailing taboos against saying some things or expressing some feelings. The response without the student's name on it then may be dealt with while the respondent need not defend it, speak to it, or be identified with it in any way unless he chooses to.

Also, a response made by one student may be seen as important or interesting by other students who did not think of it. It would be too bad, by putting a badge of ownership on a particular response, to make other students feel that they may not view it as their own or to make them feel as if they must come up with "their own" answers before they feel committed to study the subject.

Numbering responses may, by implication, be viewed as establishing a hierarchy of importance. Since some of the most significant answers in a problem census come only after long silences and when many of the most obvious answers have been quickly reeled off, such an implication of relative importance is not justified.

The teacher should not worry about writing carefully. An important part of the problem census process is pacing. The responses must be recorded quickly so that the whole thing does not bog down in impatience and boredom. We must get the responses as soon as the pupils think of them, or we will lose many of them to second thoughts, loss of courage or just annoyance at having to wait too long. The teacher should bear in mind that the whole list will be duplicated and distributed, so there should be no concern with handwriting or neatness.

Similarly, it is not a good idea to let a student record the responses. For one thing, why exclude a student from the process? He should participate with his classmates. For another, students may make a to-do about incorrect grammar, unorthodox responses, and so on. If the teacher is recording, he can make it clear by his behavior and manner that all responses are equally acceptable.

Sometimes a teacher will want to ask a problem census question and then tell the children to write down their individual responses at their seats. This defeats a number of purposes of the problem census. The creative aspect of the process, during which children hear responses they have never thought of which inspire them to think of novel responses of their own, is lost when each child works alone. Also, unless the teacher acts as recorder in full view of the class, she does not have the opportunity to establish a nonevaluative, accepting atmosphere. Having the children work individually reinforces the pattern of noncooperative, and even competitive, learning, and loses a natural opportunity for utilizing another style of teaching.

Rationale for the Use of the Problem Census

Student-Teacher Planning

There is much talk these days about the importance of permitting students to participate in planning what they will study in school. It is only in such student-teacher planning that we begin to deal realistically with the problem of motivation to learn in school. Too often the motivation phase of a school lesson takes the form of exhortation, preaching to young people that "when you go out into the world, you'll find out how important it is for you to have learned what I am trying to teach you."

The "now generation" looks with a jaundiced eye on such exhortation. They want to be interested *now;* they want to participate *now;* they are living *now* and they want to make the most of it. We can no longer sell the idea that school is merely preparation for life. School is living, and now is important.

The problem census opens up an area for study and establishes a sound base for student-teacher planning. If the teacher is attuned to her pupils, she will suggest a topic that she knows they are already concerned with, and she will give them an opportunity to take a hand in planning for the systematic examination of that topic. Even kindergarten children respond to this process. Most teachers are amazed that such small children can begin to assume responsibility for their own education. As a matter of fact, it is vital that we permit them to start at a very early age. It just does not make sense to make all decisions for people until they are seventeen or eighteen, and then suddenly expect them to take over their own lives in effective and mature ways.

Teachers who want students to participate actively in the teaching-learning process often struggle with the problem of how to get students involved in learning about subjects that teachers think are important but that students never seem to bring up. First, we must bear in mind that just because a student does not bring up a topic *in class,* it does not mean that he has no interest in it. It does not take young people very long to discover that some subjects are simply not talked about with teachers, or with other adults. Who would ever say that fourteen-year-olds are not interested in sex? Yet, how many of them would suggest to the teacher that this is a subject they would like to study in school?

The problem census provides a solution to this problem, for the teacher must take the initiative by asking a question that she knows the students are interested in. She can learn about their interests in various ways: An argument or a fight in which racial epithets are used indicates a concern with race; a rumor of drug use is undoubtedly evidence of interest in the subject; and, as I have mentioned, the teacher's own knowledge of psycho-social development would make her aware of students' interest in sex at certain ages. Of course, if the teacher misjudges the interest of her students, they just will not respond to her question. Should she ask a question to which only one or two students respond, she must give them, and any others who wish it, the chance to study those topics. A problem census is a promise, and the teacher cannot decide to drop the whole subject just because she did not get one hundred percent participation.

Diagnosis of Student Needs

One of the essential functions of the teacher is to diagnose the educational needs of students. The problem census offers not only an opportunity for diagnosing needs in a particular area before the subject is taught, but it may also be used as a diagnostic instrument for assessing the progress of learning as the subject is pursued. The first census, to introduce an area of study, may contain responses that reveal only superficial knowledge, naiveté, prejudices, and other misconceptions. The second census, after two or three weeks of study, asking *"Now, what do you want to know about . . . ?"* may elicit responses on another level, more knowledgeable, more sophisticated, dealing with more subtle aspects of the subject. Thus the teacher may assess how successful the teaching has been, and what more needs to be done.

Examples of Problem Census Questions

1. What would you like to know about race? (For almost any group, given the widespread discussion of race in this country now.)
2. What racial problems do we have in the school? (For a group that has demonstrated some awareness of and concern about racial problems.)
3. What else would you like to know about the first Black

people to come to this country? (For a group that has already spent some time studying race relations. A similar question can be asked about other groups.)

4. What drug problems do we have in this city? (Perhaps particularly fruitful after a drug incident that has been widely reported in the media.)

5. What problems are there in the club program? (Appropriate if you have some inkling of dissatisfaction concerning extracurricular activities.)

6. What problems does the other race (or "do the other races") have in school? (For a one-race group in a school with pupils of more than one race.)

7. What problems does your own race have in school? (For a one-race group in a school with pupils of more than one race.)

8. What racial problems are there in your neighborhood? (Or what racial problems are there in the neighborhood of the school?) (One-race neighborhoods may perceive no racial problems unless an interracial incident has occurred. However, children in a school that feeds from several neighborhoods may be aware of some problems; for example, they may walk to school through neighborhoods housing another race.)

9. What do you want to know about sex? (This is for any age group, since all young people have, at the very least, heard the word and wondered about it.)

10. What do you want to know about drugs? (To teach to the level of the student, rather than engaging in an intensive program on "drug abuse," thus setting the stage for adult preaching and giving answers when no questions have been asked.)

Some Experiences in Administering the Problem Census

Teachers Working for Advanced Degrees

"What do you want to know about intergroup education?"

This question was asked of twenty working teachers enrolled for a course in Intergroup Education at Temple University. People enroll for the course for a variety of reasons, ranging all the way from the need for three semester hours in order to get a salary increment to a deep commitment to intergroup education and a sincere desire to learn how to teach intergroup relations. Many of them come with the idea that "intergroup" means small-group classroom management, or general relationships between pupils and teachers, or family relations, this despite a clear course description that appears in the University's graduate catalogue.

Consequently, when the students were assembled, I "reminded" them that intergroup education, for the purposes of our course, dealt primarily with problems of race, religion, and national origin. Then I asked the problem census question and recorded the following responses:

> I'd like to know how best a "middle class white" can work with or teach to lower middle class Blacks.
>
> I have a different problem. How do you teach the Black experience without insulting or losing the whites?
>
> Blacks should not be capitalized.
>
> I want to know what the value is of relating my educational experience to my teaching experience.
>
> When the subject matter is not related to the group you are teaching, what steps should be taken?
>
> How can one teach Black history (being a Black) without creating more hostility toward whites?
>
> Can a white teach Black history effectively or honestly?
>
> How can the different languages of the intergroup effectively be mixed?
>
> How can you make upper middle class white children become aware of minority groups when there are no minority groups in their class?
>
> How can you counteract community and parental opposition to teach intergroup education to young children?
>
> Can the intergroup be treated as a group?
>
> What are the various definitions of intergroup education?
>
> What is the difference between intergroup and intragroup?
>
> How do we evaluate our effectiveness when teaching intangibles? (Intergroup type)
>
> How can you teach religious literature like the Bible without letting your own prejudices affect the literature?

What is it like to be a Black person?

How can one produce within students a "trust" and "respect" for a teacher?

The feeling I got from the group was one of considerable constraint and discomfort, which probably accounts for the limited number of responses. (The whole census took twenty minutes.) I think much of the tension resulted from the sudden realization that the subject of study was to be race relations. This has happened before. However, after several weeks of dealing with the census responses in class, a second problem census has resulted in much broader participation and demands for studying race relations on a significantly more affective level.

(It may be noted that with teachers whose immediate concerns involved problems of relationships between different nationality groups, or between old-timers and newcomers, or between religious groups, more of the responses would probably reflect those concerns.)

Fourth Grade

This is an analysis of a problem census taken by a fourth-grade teacher:

> The following problem census question was presented to my fourth grade class. In the class are twenty-nine children; twenty-eight are Black and one is Puerto Rican. The group has been working on a Black History unit entitled "From Before Slavery to Black is Beautiful" since October. This question was designed to find out what else they want to consider in their study: "What do you want to know about Black History?"
>
> At first the children volunteered questions related to topics we had already discussed. (I sensed that they felt these were the desired responses.) Soon they began to extend their thinking. They mentioned current issues as well as curiosity about past experiences.
>
> The session lasted about thirty-five minutes with only one short pause before the final silence. A little more than two-thirds of the class participated, and all showed an interest in what was happening. They were enthusiastic about their questions but sometimes made sounds if they didn't think a question was good.

Following the session when I explained the purpose of our listing, they were anxious to add more questions.

I found the experience self-motivating as well as motivating for the children. I was more relaxed in the format of accepting all responses without commenting or restructuring for a specific concept. My silence lent itself to mental planning as I wrote the questions. Recording the responses verbatim led me to think about what the child really had on his mind, rather than what I could do with his words to make them adapt to my curriculum.

WHAT DO YOU WANT TO KNOW ABOUT BLACK HISTORY?

What did the man do? (pointing to a picture of Benjamin Banneker)

About the man with the green shirt. (Frederick Douglass)

How did all the Black people get free?

About Harriet Tubman.

About Richard Allen.

How does Black people and white people get to be friends?

Why do the Black people fight the white people?

How come nobody elects a Black person for the President?

Who was the first Black American?

Why don't they want the slaves to learn how to read?

Why didn't they want that man (pointing to picture of Frederick Douglass) to read?

Why do they think one another is dumb?

How did they get their stuff to make their houses?

How come everybody's color skin have to be different?

How did they manage to escape from slavery?

When did slavery start?

Why did they sell the people on the what-cha-ma-call-it they stood on?

How come the Black people don't fight the white people?

Why can't Black and white people get together?

Why couldn't Black and white go to the same school?

Why did the white people let him (pointing to picture of

Frederick Douglass) teach everybody how to read?

How come Martin Luther King became famous?

Why did they take Black people from Africa?

How come the Black people and white people was fighting?

Why did they let the other slaves stay there and other ones run away?

Why do Black people fight against each other?

Why can't the Black people and white people get together?

Why does David take people's words out they mouth?

Why is Black people and white people so ridiculous?

Why don't the Black people and white people get together in groups?

If some African people have wives, why do they have to marry over and over?

Why did the white people be able to sit in the front of the bus and Black people have to sit in the back?

Why can't white and Black people buy their clothes?

Why do they (pointing to Puerto Rican boy) cook their eggs half done?

Why don't Black people understand Spanish and white people don't understand English?

Aw, Miss Seed knows English!

Why can't Black and white people get together and have some fun?

Why do colored people and white people fight?

Why do people over in Africa eat snakes?

Why does Black people fight white people?

Who was the first one (Black) on earth?

Why did the white people want the Black people to work for them?

Why did a white man kill Martin Luther King?

Seventh Grade

Here is a problem census taken with a seventh grade. There are Black and white children in the class, the whites largely children of working-class Italians. The community makes periodic public protestations that all races live together in harmony. Just as periodically there are outbreaks of violence between whites and Blacks. The school administrators maintain that there are no race problems in the school.

WHAT WOULD YOU LIKE TO KNOW ABOUT RACE RELATIONS?

How many races are there? How many colors are there? What was the first color?

How come Blacks marry whites?

What causes different skin colors?

Where do white people come from? Where do Black people come from?

How did discrimination against races start?

Why do white people treat Blacks as degenerates?

Why do they call white people Caucasians?

Why do they call Black people niggers?

Why did Black people have to slave for white people?

Why do people say Italians are dirtier than Negroes?

Why do white people eat cock?

Why do whites hate Blacks?

Why do white people wear funny clothes? Like a blue tie, a green shirt and corduroy pants?

How come white people get bumps around their mouth? Why do they get acne easier than Black people do?

Why do white men wear long hair? Why is white peoples' hair a different texture and why does it grow faster? Why do Black people have kinky hair?

How come white people stink?

Why do white people have pointy noses?

Why do whites get more diseases than Black?

Why is more white people retarded than Black?

How come they never pick a Black President of the United States?

How come whitey are so rich and Blacks are so poor?
Why are white babies born with bald heads and big heads?
Are colored people really trying to get ahead?

Apparently, the children used the occasion of the census to insult each other, actually engaging in a discussion under the guise of responding to the census question. The teacher was struck speechless at the evidence of interracial animosity, a factor that enabled him to get a valid census. When he recovered, he was for a long time overwhelmed with the magnitude of the problem he had discovered, before he sat down to make plans for doing something about it.

One of the things he eventually realized was that it is among the poor and among low-economic working-class people that inter-group hostilities are most often articulated. It is here that people of different racial and nationality groups most often make contact in personal ways on a day to day basis. They live in the same or adjoining neighborhoods and they often go to the same schools. The frustrations of being poor in an affluent society, the irritability resulting from crowdedness, the real or imagined competition for scarce jobs all add to the difficulties inherent in any sustained human interaction. So the arguments of childhood become intensified by the racial and ethnic animosities in the country, the competitions of youth erupt into intergroup violence, and the disagreements between neighbors are voiced as condemnations of whole groups.

The job of the teacher faced with these conditions is monumental. To help the children develop ego strength in the face of fear of other groups, to convince them of the importance of certain learnings when their daily perceptions deny any such importance—these are educational goals that must undergird any "achievement" in reading or mathematics. The teacher who took the problem census began to learn this from his children.

2

The Affective Discussion

Description of the Technique

The teacher asks eight or nine pupils to participate in a discussion while the rest of the class is engaged in other work. The selected pupils form a small circle, sitting as close to each other as possible. (There are several reasons for making sure they are seated in a tight circle: the arrangement reduces the need to speak loudly in order to make one's self heard and so helps to lower the noise level in the room; the feeling of physical closeness seems to engender an air of confidentiality that encourages the expression of feelings; it is more difficult for individuals who are physically close to remove themselves psychologically from the discussion by not speaking and/or not listening.)

The teacher, providing opportunity for discussing items from the problem census (see the Seventh Grade Problem Census, the seventh and thirteenth items on the list) says: "On the Problem Census you asked, 'Why do white people treat Blacks as degenerates?' and 'Why do whites hate Blacks?' Let's talk now about how the other race feels about your race." We are assuming that there are both Black and white pupils in the group. If the group is made up of Black youngsters only, the teacher asks, "How do white people feel about Black people?" And the reverse if all the youngsters are white. (If the problem census question has been asked in a region where the intergroup problems occur between Indian and white children, or between Mexican and Anglo children, or between Japanese-Americans and whites, then the responses will reflect concern with the groups involved. The affective discussion question, then, should deal with the appropriate groups.)

The teacher then listens to the discussion from outside the circle, offering an occasional freeing comment when it is needed, and refraining from making inhibiting comments.

Rationale for Use of the Affective Discussion

Freeing the Student to Express His Feelings

There is evidence that a significant proportion of teachers at all levels avoid dealing with emotional subjects in the classroom. Consequently, young people learn early that expression of strong feeling does not contribute to success in school. They naturally also learn that certain subjects associated with strong feelings are not appropriate for classroom discussion. Thus, by teacher choice and pupil understanding, subjects like race, sex, and until recently, drug use, were not a part of the regular curriculum. Where these subjects are included, they are treated almost exclusively on a cognitive level, with the teacher providing "facts" and an occasional hortatory lecture on what one ought not to do. Just what the pupils *feel* about race and drugs, only they know.

Almost inevitably, then, the facts are indifferently taken in and tentatively recalled for tests, and the exhortation falls on deaf, or often cynical ears. I think it is almost axiomatic that, unless we know what the students are feeling, we will not know what they need to learn. They may pass our tests with all the right answers, and then go off and continue to do what they have always done. They may be beset with problems that they cannot solve, and that a collection of facts alone cannot help them solve. (*We* have many of the facts, but we have not solved most of the problems of society.

As a matter of fact, problems proliferate as the body of fact grows.)

Sharing Differential Feelings

Youngsters of all ages need opportunity to get all their feelings about drugs, for example, out in the open, before they can begin systematically to try to solve their drug problems. There is no doubt that they have feelings about this; few parents have not been exposed to an explosive "You don't understand!" from agitated youngsters. However, like most of us, young people often think that their own feelings and those of their close friends are feelings held by "everyone." We all have a tendency to believe that our attitudes are universally shared. At the same time, if we have doubts about the validity of certain beliefs in the face of what seems like universal acceptance of them, we are often reluctant to voice those doubts. The need to be popular, to be liked, to be one of the crowd, often makes us close our minds to whatever questions are raised. If the teacher can encourage the free sharing of feelings in a relatively safe atmosphere, then a variety of attitudes may be revealed for consideration and examination. Instead of the unquestioning acceptance of one way of feeling, young people may be surprised to learn that even among their own peers there is not that uniformity of outlook that they imagined there was.

Reducing Isolation

Those young people who resolutely keep their own counsel because they believe they stand alone against the popular acceptance of drugs, of prejudice, and of patterns of sexual behavior, may discover that there are other people who feel the way they do if they are given opportunity to say how they really feel. Thus, a child who feels the need to reject the use of marijuana for health reasons may discover that he need not relinquish all claim to a place in the contemporary mainstream, that there are others who share his feelings and would like to join forces with him. His personal fight to resist the pressure to conform, then, need not be carried on in isolation. He need not be the oddball, the outsider, the one who is different. He can find strength in identification with other like-minded youngsters.

Eliminating Secrecy

It has always seemed to me that if we were to identify the major impediment in our society to the solution of our most serious problems, it would be secrecy. Government officials insist upon keeping information from the people, and so drive us into decisions based on rumor and ignorance laced with the fears and anxieties generated by distortions of reality. Similarly, parents and other adults, engaging in a conspiracy of silence regarding race, sex, and drugs, have encouraged the rapid development of a "youth culture," which is itself dedicated to keeping secrets from adults.

There are still parents who really believe that if the movie industry rates its films to exclude youngsters, that their children will not be concerned about sex. There are still politicians who really believe that laws against pornography will keep sex literature out of the hands of children. And the children keep their secret, and the generation gap widens.

There can be no solution of the problems that beset us as long as 1) much of our energy goes to keeping the problems under wraps and 2) we permit self-appointed guardians to keep all segments of the population from dealing openly with the problems. It is quite clear that to date the problems have not been solved by censorship, secrecy, denial, or prayer. We had better open them up for consideration by everyone.

Linking Up Affect and Cognition

The traditional realm of the school has been the cognitive. Teachers generally see themselves as dispensers of information, information that pupils must learn if they are to be labelled successful. It is quite possible that the increasingly large numbers of children who are unsuccessful in school, the thousands who drop out, and the tens of thousands who merely see it through in boredom and disenchantment are all reacting to the school situation that stresses the cognitive and ignores and suppresses the affective. We seem to be saying to the young people, "When you come into the classroom and close the door behind you, you must leave emotion outside. Everything that makes life frightening, exciting, joyful or anxiety-producing has no place in the classroom. Here we deal in facts, names and dates, math processes and chronologies." All the injunctions to "teach the whole child" that we learned in our Education courses go by the board in our pressure to "cover the curriculum."

The affective discussion begins to give recognition to the pupils' feelings. It makes the expression of strong feeling acceptable in the classroom setting, and it sets the groundwork for learning that people's acceptance or rejection of factual data is inescapably linked to their feelings.

Freeing the Student from Teacher Evaluation

In working with teachers I have found a behavior that is so common among them that it leads me to think that it is a behavior they first learn in school and then reinforce when they begin to teach. Teachers are reluctant to participate in a group for fear of being judged by the teacher or leader and by their peers. It is almost as if they learned as children that someone always says "That's right" or "That's wrong" when they speak. From observation in classrooms, it is evident that *they* always say "That's right" or "That's wrong" (or something to imply this) when a child speaks. The result seems to be that, when they are in a group, they are overcome by a feeling of vulnerability that inhibits free and open discussion.

It is interesting to sit in a teachers' meeting, during which the principal reads his agenda, the principal "covers" the agenda, and the teachers sit quietly, just listening. When the meeting is over, then the *real* meeting begins. In two and threes, in the corridors, in the lunchroom, and on the way home, the teachers express their dissatisfaction, pose alternative solutions to problems, and express resistance to the principal's ideas. But little of all this ever gets to the ears of the principal or is ever implemented, and what we have is a perpetual and circular gripe session. When teachers take courses, they rationalize their nonparticipation by assuring the instructor that they learn just as much by sitting quietly and "absorbing" what's going on.

Children in school are also often conditioned to this pattern of response. They are so accustomed to hearing the teacher approve or disapprove of everything they say that when they encounter an adult who just listens non-committally they often feel that the adult's silence is the result of determined effort to restrain strong disapproval!

The affective discussion, then, is in part an opportunity to permit the child to say whatever he has to say without being evaluated by the teacher. Perhaps if the teacher does not so constantly assume the role of the evaluator, the children will not demonstrate this behavior in their relations with each other. With help (see the Four-Stage Rocket) they may even learn to listen to each other and build on each other's contributions, instead of rejecting out of hand what a person has to say or accepting it only if it agrees with their own point of view.

Educating for the Future, Not Perpetuating the Past

There is one factor in solving the problems of race, drug use and relationship between sexes that teachers especially often do not consider. Because we largely see ourselves as disseminators of information, we forget that we simply do not have the answers to many of our current problems. We are learning that a significant part of what we "teach" must include opportunities and skills so that a new generation may discover some of the answers we need. Teaching children to interact with each other, listen to each other, to be honest and open as they work together are goals consistent with this new awareness. We are, in effect, being called upon to free the children from ourselves, since we and most of our generation have been locked into old perceptions of problems and old solutions that do not work.

Small-Group Interaction

The experimental evidence on the value of small classes and lower pupil-teacher ratios is sparse and conflicting. There are some data that indicate teachers teach exactly the same way whether their classes are large or small. However, common sense tells us that if there are fifteen children in a class, they will probably have more opportunity to interact with the teacher than would a class of thirty-five.

The question arises, "Why is it so important for the children to interact with the teacher?" It is mostly with each other that they must learn to live and to work effectively. It is in concert with members of their own generation that they will have to find solutions to the problems of life. It is from each other that they need acceptance and recognition. And it is in each other's eyes that they see the signs of their own success or failure. The best that the good teacher can do is provide opportunity for children to become active, productive, cooperating members of their own society.

The small-group, affective discussion is an activity that encourages children to put their feelings into words, accept each other's feelings, compare emotional experiences, and learn to see their peers, even in the school setting, as more than just reciters of facts.

Often the teacher is afraid that the interaction of the affective discussion will erupt into physical violence. Generally, she is not so concerned that this will actually occur in the classroom, where she is present to maintain order, but outside the school, where adult controls are absent. We cannot rule that out as a possibility, but I think it would be difficult to determine which of the numerous after-school fights are attributable to participation in affective discussion in class. As a matter of fact, interracial conflicts among young people usually occur when honest, open communication across race lines is nonexistent. The chances are that such communication will immeasurably decrease the need for physical violence as a response to the frustrations and hostilities generated by the proximity of the races.

Learning to Conduct an Affective Discussion: A Game

Some time ago, after I was convinced of the importance of providing pupils with opportunity to discuss emotional subjects, I realized that teachers, often without realizing it, actually said things in the course of a discussion that inhibited the pupils and made them reluctant to continue to speak. Teachers also said things that apparently had a freeing effect on the pupils and encouraged them to participate in the discussion and keep it going. I began to identify these freeing and inhibiting responses and to observe their effect on very young children, older children and adults. A common pattern of responses to these teacher comments began to emerge, with people of all ages reacting in similar ways.

When I had collected all the teacher comments I had been hearing, I asked a group of people who had had years of experience in conducting discussions, primarily in race relations, to determine the freeing and inhibiting qualities of the teacher comments. On the basis of our cumulative experience and common judgment, we rated each comment freeing or inhibiting on a 60-point scale.

Teachers who want to learn what they may say and what they must not say in the course of conducting an affective discussion may play a game I devised. A group of eight or nine people use a set of cards. On each card is written a teacher comment. Most teachers will recognize the comments as the sort of things teachers often say in the classroom. Most of us have used them at one time or another, usually without any profound analysis of their effect on pupils.

Also on each card is a value. The values range from −30 (indicating the most inhibiting teacher response) to +30 (indicating the most freeing teacher response). Between the two extremes, the comments are valued in multiples of five. For example, +25 indicates very freeing, −15 indicates rather inhibiting, and so on. There are no 0 values, since zero means the response to the comment is usually neutral, and we were not concerned with comments that seemed to make no difference to the discussion.

One person at a time turns up a card and reads the teacher comment aloud to the rest of the group. Everyone then guesses if the response is freeing or inhibiting, and just how freeing or inhibiting they think it is (on the 60-point scale). (The players must bear in mind that each comment is evaluated in terms of its effect in a specific situation: a group of youngsters are discussing "What do you think Black people feel about white people?" or "How do you feel about smoking pot?" or "How do you feel about sexual relations between high school students?"). Each player puts his guess in the Guessed Value column on the score sheet. The player with the card then reads aloud the value on the card, and each player puts that real value in the Real Value column on the score sheet. After everyone has finished castigating the judges who put the value on the comment, each player scores the round by computing the difference in points between the guessed and the real values, and adding or subtracting 20 depending on whether or not they accurately guessed the remark was freeing or inhibiting.

Thus, a player who guesses a remark is very freeing, +25, and discovers it is extremely inhibiting, −30, is 55 points off the mark and must put −55 in the Score column. Then, because he guessed it was freeing when it was actually inhibiting, he loses another 20 points. His score for that round, then, is −75.

Now comes the most important part of the game: the players must discuss the basis of their own valuations and try to determine the basis of the judges' values. (If there is a teacher-education faculty member conducting the group, he makes himself available to give additional information as it is needed. The discussion which follows should help to clarify the basis for the values by detailing the judges' experiences in conducting and observing affective discussions.)

When the group feels that it has discussed the response adequately, the next player reads a card and the process is continued.

Sample Card for Game

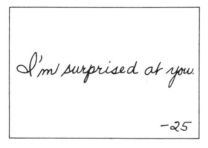

At the end, each person finds his score by taking the last ten scores in the Score column, adding the pluses, adding the minuses, and getting the difference between the two sums. (The reason for using the last ten scores lies in the assumption that the longer one plays the game, the more accurate will his valuations be. So a player's best scores should be found toward the end of the game.)

Sometimes a person discovers that his first few scores are very high, and then get lower as he continues to play. The explanation seems to lie in the fact that often a teacher makes remarks in terms of his feelings, which are responsive to the feelings of pupils. Without really understanding why, he feels that "I know you don't mean that" is an inhibiting thing to say to someone who has just said something emotional. However, as the discussion of the players continues and information is exchanged, a player trying to integrate the information with his intuitive responses may become confused.

Score Sheet for Affective Discussion Game

Guessed Value	Real Value	Score (No. of points separating the Guessed Value from the Real Value + or − 20 points)

For a while, his guesses may reflect that confusion, until he is able to use the additional information he is getting and refine his guesses.

If more than one group is playing, they may want to compare group scores. In that case, the players in each group add their final scores and divide by the number of players to get the group score.

Handouts for Teachers Learning to Conduct an Affective Discussion

LEADING AN AFFECTIVE DISCUSSION (ON RACE RELATIONS)

The Question

Offers opportunity for expression of feeling and opinion. Relates to the experiences of the group. Does not require a "right" answer.

The Teacher

The following teacher behaviors are roughly evaluated on a scale of +5 to +30 for more freeing responses and −5 to −30 for more inhibiting responses:

1. That's right. −25
2. That's wrong. −25
3. Don't you mean people aren't kind to each other? −25
4. That's not a nice thing to say. −25
5. Gasp! −25
6. Good. −25
7. Look that up in your history book for tomorrow. −15
8. Now, that isn't what I told you last time. −25
9. We don't use such words here. −25
10. I'm surprised at you. −25
11. I know you don't mean that. −25
12. The fact is that Lincoln freed the slaves. (or: The fact is that Custer and his men were massacred by the Indians.) −25
13. We treat everyone alike, regardless of race, creed, or color. −15
14. There is no such fact in history. −20
15. Where did you get that information? −20
16. Can you prove that? −25
17. What do you think? (To a child who has asked the teacher a question) +25
18. How do you feel? (To the group) +30

19. I agree. — 20
20. I disagree. — 25
21. That's nonsense. — 30
22. Yes? (To the group, after an extended silence) +25
23. Does anyone else have anything to say? +10
24. How does this relate to what we were discussing yesterday? — 5
25. How does this relate to the chapter on the American Revolution in History books? — 15
26. Stupid! — 30
27. Now, that makes sense. — 25
28. Let him finish his thought. +15
29. Isn't anyone going to answer his question? — 10
30. Are you all going to ignore what he said? — 10
31. Now, let's discuss that point for a few minutes. — 25
32. I won't have that here. — 30
33. Oh, is that so? — 20
34. Are you saying that George Washington doesn't deserve the title of Father of Our Country? — 25
35. Don't say such things unless you really know. — 30
36. (Silence without facial expression) +30
37. If you can't behave, we'll stop this right now. — 25
38. Close that book while we're discussing. — 15
39. (Repeating a child's comment without emotion or comment of your own.) (Only after extended silence) +25
40. One more remark like that, and we go back to doing arithmetic! — 30
41. It's all right to say what you feel. +30
42. It's all right to say what you think. +30
43. How many agree with that? Raise your hands. — 30
44. How many disagree with that? Raise your hands. — 30
45. Everybody doesn't have to agree. +20
46. That's why Johnny gets A's on his papers. — 25
47. You don't know how to have a mature discussion. This is the last time we'll try anything like this. — 30
48. Raise your hand and wait to be called on. — 15
49. I want silence unless you're reciting. — 30
50. Stand and speak in complete sentences. — 30
51. I don't know. +30
52. I won't answer any questions during this discussion. +30

53. We mustn't get excited. — 30
54. We must be polite to each other. — 25
55. We must be ladies and gentlemen. — 25
56. (Interjecting another question.) — 25

LEADING AN AFFECTIVE DISCUSSION (ON DRUG USE)

The Question

Offers opportunity for expression of feeling and opinion. Relates to the experiences of the group. Does not require a "right" answer.

The Teacher

The following teacher behaviors are roughly evaluated on a scale of +5 to +30 for more freeing responses and —5 to —30 for more inhibiting responses:

1. That's right. — 25
2. That's wrong. — 25
3. Don't you mean people aren't kind to each other? — 25
4. That's not a nice thing to say. — 25
5. Gasp! — 25
6. Good. — 25
7. Look that up in the reference book I gave you. — 15
8. Now, that isn't what I told you last time. — 25
9. We don't use such words here. — 25
10. I'm surprised at you. — 25
11. I know you don't mean that. — 25
12. The fact is that people die of heroin every day. — 20
13. There is no such fact in science. — 20
14. Where did you get that information? — 25
15. Can you prove that? — 25
16. What do you think? (To a pupil who has asked the teacher a question) +25
17. How do you feel? (To the group) +30
18. I agree. — 25
19. I disagree. — 25
20. That's nonsense. — 30

21. Yes? (To the group, after an extended silence) +25
22. Does anyone else have anything to say? +10
23. How does this relate to what we were discussing yesterday? — 5
24. The fact is that using marijuana is against the law. — 20
25. Stupid. — 30
26. Now, that makes sense. — 25
27. Let him finish his thought. +15
28. Isn't anyone going to answer his question? — 10
29. Are you all going to ignore what he said? — 10
30. Now, let's discuss that point for a few minutes. — 25
31. I won't have that here. — 30
32. Oh, is that so? — 20
33. Are you saying that you think it's all right to smoke marijuana? — 25
34. Don't say such things unless you really know. — 30
35. (Silence without facial expression) +30
36. If you can't behave, we'll stop this right now. — 25
37. Close that book while we're discussing. — 15
38. (Repeating a child's comment without emotion or comment of your own.) (Only after extended silence) +25
39. One more remark like that, and we go back to doing arithmetic. — 30
40. It's all right to say what you feel. +30
41. It's all right to say what you think. +30
42. How many agree with that? Raise your hands. — 30
43. How many disagree with that? Raise your hands. — 30
44. Everybody doesn't have to agree. +20
45. That's why John gets A's on his papers. — 25
46. You don't know how to have a mature discussion. This is the last time we'll try anything like this. — 30
47. Raise your hand and wait to be called on. — 15
48. I want silence unless you're reciting. — 30
49. Stand and speak in complete sentences. — 30
50. I don't know. +30
51. I won't answer any questions during this discussion. +30
52. We mustn't get excited. — 30
53. We must be polite to each other. — 25
54. We must be ladies and gentlemen. — 25
55. (Interjecting another question.) — 25

The Freeing and Inhibiting Teacher Responses

In terms of the effect of the teacher response, "That's right," on the development of an affective discussion, we say it is generally inhibiting. Teachers often find it difficult to accept this valuation, and understandably so. We know that it is good to give positive support to a child. "That's right" is a nice thing to say; it bolsters the child's conception of himself and encourages him to continue making contributions. Yet here we say it is inhibiting.

We must emphasize that we do not suggest that teachers discontinue saying "That's right" to children. We strongly urge, however, that they refrain from doing so during an affective discussion. Though the immediate effect of such encouragement on a specific child may be positive, what effect may it have on the children in the group who disagree with him, and with the teacher? How encouraged will they be to state a diametrically opposed point of view? Also, how about the complimented child? Should he later find himself changing his mind, will he feel free to say, in effect, that he now feels the teacher is wrong?

There is another factor that should be borne in mind, a factor we often overlook because it comes into direct conflict with most teachers' perception of the teacher role. We usually see ourselves as dispensers of information. In most classrooms, though teachers may not say this is their function, it is clear that the aim of teaching is to see to it that pupils retain a body of "facts." The cold fact is, however, that in the areas of race relations, drug use, and, probably, sex, teachers are no experts. Most adults are obviously not experts in these areas. If they were, we would not be beset with the problems that are tearing us apart as a society; we would be solving those problems!

Our job is to help rear a generation of people who know more than we do, who are free from our fears and anxieties and misconceptions concerning race, drugs, and sex. When the teacher says "That's right," she may just as easily be wrong as right, so the first thing we must do is detach the pupils from our conception of right in these areas, and leave them free to find out for themselves.

Even if we are right, we may never know just what it is that students need to know if we do not leave them free to say whatever they think and feel. As the teacher listens to the affective discussion without imposing his ideas of right and wrong on it, he can learn much about what his students need to learn, and he can begin to plan opportunities for them to add to their knowledge and experience, to correct misconceptions, and to increase skills in human interaction.

Other responses, like "That's wrong," "Good," "I'm surprised at you," "I agree," "I disagree," "Now, that makes sense," and "That's why Johnny gets A's on his papers," are all evaluated on the same basis. They impose the teacher's values and information on the group and they tend to inhibit opposing points of view.

Teachers will recognize most of the following responses as attempts to teach children good interpersonal relations: "Don't you mean people aren't kind to each other?" "That's not a nice thing to say," "We must be polite to each other," "We must be ladies and gentlemen." These attempt to establish a standard of politeness in interaction, an etiquette in discussion that is not related to the feelings of the participants. As so much of the code of etiquette implies, we are not to say anything that disturbs the surface calm, we are not to make others uncomfortable, we are to say only what everyone is prepared to accept. For generations, this code has contributed to the apparent ennui of most Americans in the face of proliferating social problems. For years people maintained, in all honesty, that there were no racial problems, that America was a country without chronic hunger, that rebellion was merely a function of adolescence and was resolved with developing maturity. And all the time, "nice" people were polite to each other and kept their voices down.

Now, we want to teach young people to interact with each other and still express themselves freely. We want them to bring their strongest feelings out and examine them in the light of other people's honesty. We want the fears and anxieties dealt with, not repressed and converted into guilts and hostilities. I decline to argue the value of politeness in casual social situations, but there can be no doubt that, in encouraging affective discussion in the classroom, the traditional admonitions to be polite must be abandoned.

More clearly antithetical to the goals of free and open discussion is such a teacher response as "We mustn't get excited." Obviously, if people are going to express their feelings on subjects about which there is strong feeling, getting excited is inevitable. It simply does not make sense to discuss such subjects *without* getting excited. Unless the hates and angers are released, there can be no aftermath of calm consideration of solutions. Of course, if we are caught in the meshes of the idea that the good teacher has a quiet class, then we need to work this out for ourselves, and with our administrators.

What are the limits of permissible excitement in the classroom? I have my own limit; I do not permit pupils to hit each other. This may be an adult bias, or even a middle class one. However, the several thousands of affective discussions I have led and observed have resulted in only two physical lunges, both of which were neatly intercepted and turned aside.

Some teachers feel that obscene language (and obscenity is differentially defined!) should be prohibited. Such teachers, while not questioning the inhibiting values put on the following responses, still justify this kind of inhibition as necessary in the classroom. They feel the need to say such things as, "I won't have that here," "One more remark like that, and we go back to doing arithmetic," "We don't use such words here." Or they just gasp when they hear certain words, as if they had never heard them before.

The belief that people should learn to express themselves without obscene language is, perhaps, laudable as a goal. Certainly, people should have at their command so many words that they are not compelled, through ignorance, to rely only on obscenities. However, if we honestly want youngsters to say what they feel, we must leave the choice of language to them, and leave the lessons in propriety and vocabulary for another time. Can you imagine yourself finally being able to express a festering anger, "You white bastards think you own the world!" and being admonished for not saying it in more proper language? The resultant feeling may very well be, "Why try to be honest? The objectives are still to be nice and polite and don't rock the boat!"

The information-giving function of the teacher again comes into play with such responses as, "The fact is that Lincoln freed the slaves," and "There is no such fact in science." Again remembering that the teacher's "facts" may be errors, and that the insistence on the acceptance of these facts will undoubtedly inhibit expressions of doubt, denial and rejection, it is better for the teacher to suspend this function during the affective discussion. The teacher's "facts" are very often the material to be found in "accepted" textbooks. This accounts for such responses as, "Look that up in your history book for tomorrow," and "How does this relate to the chapter on the American Revolution in our history books?" Again and again in recent years it has been pointed out to teachers that the "facts" in the school books are not accurate. In the area of race relations, the omissions and distortions and outright lies are numerous. In drug use, the materials are as likely to be based on the author's conception of morality or on his fear as they are on fact. The same may be said of school books dealing with sex. The children often have more facts than the books do. Certainly many of them are having experiences that some adult writers have never dreamed of! There is a cynicism concerning school and adults that develops when real life gives the lie to the collection of "facts" we teach. (Is this cynicism what we are calling the generation gap?)

When the teacher controls the direction of the discussion, he is inhibiting the students' own control. When the teacher says, "Now, that isn't what I told you the last time," he is insisting that the discussion deal with recall of specific data, instead of with the feelings of the moment, to say nothing of the implicit demand that the students accept his point of view! The same is true with "How does this relate to what we were discussing yesterday?" (though this does not have the same implied evaluation). This is not to say that the teacher should not help the pupil relate past experiences to the present, or information obtained in one situation with other information. The point is that this is not the time to do it, when we are trying to free the pupil from intellectual constraints so that he may begin to deal with his feelings.

Teacher control becomes apparent in many responses: "Isn't anyone going to answer his question?" pushes the group to consider something they may not care to at this time. The same with "Are you all going to ignore what he said?" Obviously, if the group is ignoring what he says, that is what it chooses to do, and the teacher's attempt to force it is a way of taking control. "Now, let's discuss that point for a few minutes," is a perfectly valid suggestion when the teacher is trying to lead the class to consider something he thinks is important. However, it is not justified if the major objective of the lesson is to encourage freedom of expression and direction.

The teacher's skill in asking questions sometimes betrays her, for she sees instances during the discussion when the youngsters could profit from considering certain leading questions. No matter how open the questions seem, no matter how free they appear to be from dogmatic implications, the net effect of asking additional questions in the course of the discussion is to take control away from the group and put it into the hands of the teacher. If the teacher feels the students are missing some important ideas in their discussion, later time should be provided to give them information, let them search out additional data, or have some new experiences, so that the next time they engage in affective discussion, they will have a broader cognitive base of departure.

The teacher must also try to remove from the atmosphere of the affective discussion any suggested threat of disciplinary action. There is nothing freeing about discussing a gut issue with the specter of punishment hovering over the group. "If you don't behave, we'll stop this right now," is punishment by depriving youngsters of the opportunity to get actively involved and maybe, even, get out of control in minor ways until they feel comfortable in such involvement. "One more remark like that, and we go back to doing arithmetic," is punishment by arithmetic. (Probably the largest single cause of "blocking" in the study of mathematics!)

Similar to the threat of punishment is the promise that this activity will never be permitted again: "You don't know how to have a mature discussion. This is the last time we'll try anything like this." This is a rather common teacher response to pupil behavior, and it is consistent with a widespread practice in our profession. We have a tendency to provide school activities for youngsters who have already learned the skills needed for the activities. Thus, children who are competent public speakers get the chance to make speeches. Children who can act get picked for parts in plays. Children who know how to participate in a group discussion are permitted to do so, while those who don't know how are not given the opportunity to learn. It is almost as if we expect that, with time, the skill will appear, just as with time the body grows taller.

Also similar to punishment is the psychological beating youngsters take when adults respond to their feelings with "That's nonsense," and "Stupid." It is, to say the least, impolite and, since teachers are not the ones who are practicing free expression in these discussions, they should suppress the urge to be impolite. At the other extreme, labelling a child's expression as nonsense or stupid can be destructive of his self-esteem, while it does nothing to help him see other points of view. Indeed, if his self-concept is sufficiently damaged, he will *need* prejudice and hostility to maintain the illusion that other people are less worthwhile than he is. Of course, the other children who hear these responses will usually be cautious about revealing themselves and thus risking similar denigration.

The response, "Close that book while we're discussing," has an element of disciplining in it, too, like a "naughty, naughty" or a light slap. But there may be something more significant than naughtiness in the behavior of the pupil who is apparently reading a book during the discussion, or staring out the window, or rummaging in his desk, or any one of a number of behaviors which make it clear that he is withdrawing from participation. It may be that the student is finding the discussion so disturbing that he cannot handle it and he is defending himself by withdrawing. If he is permitted to turn aside for a while without threat, the fact that the discussion is proceeding and nobody is being destroyed by it may encourage him to come back in again. The point is, he *needs* to withdraw for a while. He should be permitted to do so.

The whole idea of spontaneity and freedom in affective discussion is diluted, if not destroyed, when we insist, "Raise your hand and wait to be called on," "I want silence unless you're reciting," and "Stand and speak in complete sentences." If you have ever witnessed the ludicrous behavior of adults automatically raising their hands before they venture to speak in a group, you know the strength of this early school conditioning. People need to learn to look each other in the face and speak to each other, not to some external authority who gives permission and then approves or disapproves. This need for personal interaction in a group makes standing and speaking in complete sentences irrelevant, and makes hand-raising senseless. The need for spontaneity and feeling makes demand for absolute silence impossible to honor. (Think of any group of teachers who buzz-buzz-buzz each time a speaker says something meaningful.) It is a natural response, and interest in what is being said acts as a natural silencer while someone is speaking.

In the course of an affective discussion, when a child makes a statement, and the teacher demands, "Where did you get that information?" or "Can you prove that?" or "Don't say such things unless you really know," the teacher is, in effect, nullifying her stated objectives. Many of the things we believe, especially in an area like race relations, are not based on provable fact. Our misconceptions are bred in the home, taken in with the myriad small unremembered words and experiences that become an integral part of our total perception of life. When a child says, "Niggers are dirty," he does not know where he got that information, and he certainly is not prepared to prove it. To force him to the wall with such questions will either just shut him up, and do the same to others who have this opinion, or it will encourage them to find support for their opinion in rationalization and less subtle forms of lying. We need to hear children say these things so that we may be aware of their educational needs. If they never say what they believe, we will go on thinking they believe what we are telling them.

This is one reason for rating as inhibiting responses like "We treat everyone alike regardless of race, creed, or color." We keep telling children this and we think they believe that everyone *is* equal and is treated equally. Most children are reluctant to challenge the teacher on such a widely verbalized value. To challenge it is to hit at our American Creed. So those who know better keep their knowledge to themselves and "turn off " in school. Those whom life has sheltered from awareness of discrimination are either suddenly shockingly disillusioned later on, or they go through life with blinders, determined to see no evil, even in their own behavior.

The teacher's challenge of a student response is similar to the dissemination of facts and the imposition of values. "Oh, is that so?" and "Are you saying that you think it's all right to smoke marijuana?" are easily interpreted as a caveat to the student that he is on thin ice. Some teachers, in defense, have said that the intent here may merely be to express surprise or interest, or to ask for clarification. There is a wide margin of risk, however, that most of the participants will not interpret the responses this way. At any rate, the teacher's interest or need for clarification is not important in this process. The more he insists on focusing the attention of the group on him, the less free of his influence the group will be.

This influence may be felt when the teacher decides, at some point in the discussion, that is is time to ask the students to stand up and be counted. "How many agree with that? Raise your hands." "How many disagree with that? Raise your hands." Here again, the point is not that pupils should not take public stands on issues. As a matter of fact, specific opportunities should be made for just this sort of thing. However, whether or not this is done in the course of an affective discussion must be the decision of the students themselves. In a discussion free of outside control, only the participants may decide when they are ready to take a stand on an issue, or even if it is necessary to take a stand at all. The teacher may observe in the group a tendency to avoid owning up to a point of view, evading forthright statements, and so on. In this case, he begins to plan lessons designed to help students clarify their values and state them publicly. But this cannot be done during the discussion.

Generally, the teacher-response items with plus values have a tendency to turn the discussion back to the group when the children try to place the teacher in the role of arbitrary authority: "What do you think?" to a child who has asked the teacher a question and "How do you feel?" to the group when a child has expressed a strong feeling that seems to have shocked the rest of the children into silence.

Teacher responses like "Does anyone else have anything to say?" and "Let him finish his thought" are attempts to keep the discussion going. They have some freeing effect in that they merely encourage discussion without interjecting a teacher viewpoint. However, they are not the most desirable ways to teach children how to have a discussion. It is better to note that the pupils are reluctant to speak about some things or that they do not really listen to each other and often interrupt. Later, then, the teacher may devote some time to teaching them how to have a discussion. (See the Four-Stage Rocket, Chapter 3.)

When the teacher says, "Yes?" after an extended silence, she is trying to reassure the children that, whatever it was that silenced them, it is safe to continue the discussion, that the anxiety they feel is part of the process, that the obscenity someone has just uttered in the heat of emotion has not killed anyone.

Similarly, repeating a child's comment without emotion or comment of your own is also reassurance and encouragement to continue, especially when the child's comment has gone beyond the accepted norms of the group and everyone has fallen silent for some time. The teacher who is shocked by an obscenity or announcement of a value that she considers unacceptable must, if she does nothing else, maintain silence without facial expression. Any betrayal of her feeling at this point will merely make it clear to the students that there are some feelings they had better not reveal. Since the major objective of the affective discussion is to express feelings freely, the teacher who is still uncomfortable with the topic under discussion can best facilitate it by saying nothing.

Excerpts from Affective Discussions

Third-Graders

TEACHER: Now, you don't have to raise your hand, okay? What do you do when you want to talk?

CHILD: Just talk out.

TEACHER: That's right, you break in when you get the chance. Now what happens when two people talk at the same time?

CHILDREN: *(Several children speak at once.)*

TEACHER: Wait a minute. Do you see what happened? I couldn't understand, could I? Now, what can you do when somebody's talking? You have to wait until you can break in.

Here the teacher has prefaced a discussion on race with a brief discussion about how to have a discussion. He is helping the children identify behaviors that are more appropriate to free discussion than they are to the more formal traditional classroom structure. This kind of instruction at the beginning of an affective discussion generally has the effect of dimming enthusiasm, creating impatience (with its attendant discipline problems), and diluting the lesson's objectives.

Fourth-Graders

TEACHER: I have a sentence on the board. Can you read it?

CHILDREN: *(In unison)* A race is a group of people having a number of . . . *(silence, confusion, giggles)*

TEACHER: physical

CHILDREN: physical . . . *(confusion)*

TEACHER: characteristics

CHILDREN: characteristics in common.

A criterion of teacher behavior is that the initiating question (in this case, a statement) must be in the language of the children. Here the children cannot read the statement. It subsequently became apparent that, when the teacher read it to them, they did not understand it. Thus, before the affective discussion could start, there had to be a discussion of the meaning of the statement. By the time the meaning was clear, the children had had enough of discussion about race and were impatient to go on to something else.

First-Graders

TEACHER:	What do you think people think about race?
CLASS:	*(Long silence)*
TEACHER:	What do *you* think about race?
CLASS:	*(Long silence)*
TEACHER:	Come on, say whatever you feel like saying.
CLASS:	*(Silence)*
FIRST CHILD:	When I race, my feets hurt.
SECOND CHILD:	When some girl's mother that I go to church with, she said that some girls, they didn't never like her hair. Cause they were Spanish and she was just Puerto Rican.

This teacher starts a discussion on race with a direct question about attitudes. Though the question deals directly with the subject, it offers the children the safety of expressing what they think people's attitudes are generally. In this way, they may test the climate of acceptance before they talk about their own attitudes.

However, after he asks the question, there is a long silence. The teacher bears up under it for some time. When the silence persists he succumbs to the temptation of changing the question. With the new question, he eliminates the safety factor by making the question more personal and direct. And the silence becomes even more profound.

Finally, he discovers that at least one child does not know the meaning of the word race in this context. But another child has understood all along.

Tenth-Graders

TEACHER:	I've noticed that people of all groups live in the neighborhood around the school—Black people, Puerto Ri-

can people, and white people. Have you noticed the same thing?

STUDENTS: (Scattered responses of yes . . . yes . . .)

TEACHER: Okay. Do you mind walking through the neighborhood on your way to and from school?

STUDENTS: Yes. Yes. No.

TEACHER: Do you ever get a chance to speak to some of the people in the neighborhood?

STUDENTS: No. No. Yes.

TEACHER: Tom Farley, have you ever had any experiences with the people in the neighborhood?

An initiating question that requires a yes or no response can be self-defeating. It sets up a pattern of teacher question/student response that may be difficult to change into the student/student kind of interaction that characterizes the group discussion. After she gets an answer to her first question, the teacher must ask another question. Then another, and another. Finally, almost in desperation to get a discussion going, the teacher calls on one student and begins an interchange with him. Now the traditional pattern is reinforced and the opportunity for a group discussion is gone.

Teachers' Diagnoses

Second-Graders

I asked ten of my second-graders the question, "What do you think about Black people?" Nine of the children are Black, one is Puerto Rican. These little seven years olds had much to say. Each child talked through his own experiences with white people. Most of these experiences were negative ones. Through these experiences and those of their families, the children get their views on relations between Blacks and whites.

At first the children were a little hesitant and weren't sure what they were expected to say. Soon, however, they began speaking of their feelings and experiences. "Black people are better than white people." "Why do white people *like* to fight Black people?" The children put down white people. They are evil and always bother Black people. Whites steal from Blacks and take away their pocketbooks.

The little Puerto Rican girl surprised me. Instead of being silent, as she had been in the Problem Census, she came back at the black children. She said the white people don't bother the Black people, it's the Blacks who bother the whites. And in her immediate Black neighborhood, this has been her experience. She brings them into her house and plays with them, but in return they are not nice to her. 'Why don't Black people want to be friends with white people?' She is still white and has her own superior attitude. She even taught a Black man to speak Spanish. The Black children find this hard to believe. Only white people speak Spanish. Where she used to live in Buffalo, white and Black people were friends.

The children seem to equate white with policemen. The Black people don't do anything and the police 'mess' with them. The white police don't believe the colored people. These children have had much experience with the police through their parents and older brothers and sisters. They hear the stories of these adults and to them the policeman is a bad white man persecuting Blacks.

The children then switched to the derogatory things about white people. They are dirty and smell and they don't wear clothes. Almost each child had a story to tell about people they had seen that had only underwear on. I suppose at age seven this is a very amusing thing. They talked about Black and white children they had seen. One child came up with this interesting thought. 'The only time we be friends with white people is when we be white.'

This session with the children continued to enlighten me as to their thoughts on the problems between Blacks and whites. The children spoke their views freely and they seemed to forget that I was there. They weren't afraid to say what they wanted to. They gave each other a chance to speak. Some children also kept on the subject very well. Each time someone began to drift into another subject, another child would bring the discussion back to the subject. It seemed to me that the children handled this situation very well. Their feelings did come through. It was a very worthwhile experience for them as well as for their teacher.

Fifth-Graders

Throughout the discussion, the children had a problem using the words white and black in describing people. Quite a few times, I asked, 'Who are *they?*' One time, though, I said too much, and I feel the comment was negative. 'Let's not be afraid of using the word' (in discussing white and black). Here, I was possibly giving the children the thought that there was something wrong in using the words white and black to describe people.

I made another comment which I felt led the children. The children were talking about white store owners who took advantage of them. I asked, 'Do you get this reaction when you go into a store a black man owns?' They continued to discuss occasions where black store owners did things wrong. They probably felt these were the answers I wanted. I was more careful after that.

3

The Four-Stage Rocket

Description of the Technique

Pre-Test

Break up into groups of not more than eight.
Select an observer.
Discuss the assigned topic for five minutes. (The observer will record his evaluation of the discussion.)

Stage 1

Select a time keeper.
Continue the discussion for five minutes, strictly limiting each person's contribution to fifteen seconds.

Stage 2

Continue the discussion for five minutes, again limiting each person's contribution to fifteen seconds.

However, before a person speaks, he must wait three seconds after the previous person has finished speaking.

Stage 3

Continue the discussion for five minutes, again limiting each person's contribution to fifteen seconds and waiting the three-second interval.

In addition, no person may say what he wants to until he has accurately reflected the contribution of the person immediately preceding him.

Stage 4

Continue the discussion for five minutes. Limit each person's contribution to fifteen seconds and wait three seconds. No one may speak until he has accurately reflected and no one may speak a second time until everyone in the group has spoken.

Post-Test

Continue the discussion for 5 minutes, with no limitations on speaking. Have the same observer as in the Pre-Test record his evaluation of the discussion.

Permit the observer of each group to compare aloud the pattern of interaction of his group in the Pre-Test and in the Post-Test, and then ask the group under discussion to come to some tentative conclusions about the effect of the stages on their behavior. The chances are that they will conclude that they felt much freer in the Post-Test, with all restrictions off. This is the natural feeling of relief after a period of struggling to change accustomed behaviors. They may conclude that they need to be more careful about cutting in on each other. One person may conclude that he felt good about having an opportunity to speak, because he is usually crowded out by more aggressive speakers.

The group may conclude that they hated the whole thing. This is understandable because of the built-in causes of frustration. If the expression of rejection of the technique is very strong, it might be well to consider some of the adaptations of the technique. (See pp. 56–57.)

In the course of the discussion after the Post-Test, lead the pupils to express what they see as the purpose of each stage, and how this purpose relates to their own ideas about group discussion. Though the purposes are generally easy to see, it is well to have them verbalized, so that the pupils begin to get into the habit of looking for reasonable explanations of what they do in school. This also contributes to the development of independence and critical examination of behavior, and encourages youngsters to see school as making at least as much sense as other aspects of their lives.

Rationale for Use of the Four-Stage Rocket

Practicing Skills for Small-Group Interaction

When I teach something like the four-stage rocket, I often see clearly how a teacher's conception of education can stand in the way of her teaching effectively. Over and over again, after I have used the technique with teachers and they have in turn tried it with their children, they report that it was a "success," in which case they feel satisfied, or that it was a "failure," in which case they suggest that their children were "not ready for this," "immature," "slow," or that they "needed more preparation." It takes some time to make them realize that if it was "successful," then the children probably didn't need it in the first place, and if it was a "failure," then that was evidence that it had to be done again and again until the children learned the skills involved.

Yet this perception of teaching is not at all unusual. Especially in the area of small-group interaction, teachers are accustomed to expect children to be able to work in groups before anyone teaches them to do so. Generally, the first time a teacher decides to "break the class up into groups," she just does it. The immediate response is generally chaos. (If the chaos continues for any length of time, mayhem begins to develop.) The teacher, panic-stricken, claps everybody back into rows, and after a brief, "You don't know how to behave in small groups," she goes back to the traditional classroom pattern of children lined up facing the teacher and responding only when called on.

Why should the children be expected to know how to work in groups when they have not been taught how to do so? Should school be a place to demonstrate what you have already learned, or should it provide opportunity to learn new things? Every teacher will answer quickly that school is for learning. But, as we noted before, what we do belies what we say. The child who reads well is called on to read for the group; the "responsible" child is given prestigious jobs; *and those who know how to work in groups are permitted to do so.*

When the teacher has his first affective discussion with a group of pupils, he discovers, in addition to the need for information and correction of misconceptions, that pupils say what they think and give scant attention to what anyone else says. He hears them interrupt each other, engage in monologues, or retire into silence because they cannot get a word in. He knows that much of the value of small-group discussion lies in really hearing diverse points of view, building on the perceptions and insights of others, developing empathy with other people's lives and experiences. To give the children opportunity to practice some of the skills that are necessary if they are to participate effectively in group discussions, the teacher involves them in the Four-Stage Rocket.

The skills learned during these stages are useful in almost any kind of small-group interaction. Listening to others, letting everyone contribute, keeping one's own contributions concise and to the point, all help to keep a group moving toward its goal. Children working together to complete a mural, build a World's Fair model, or present a play need, among other skills, the ability to plan together, to build on each other's contributions, to make sure that no one is ignored or excluded just because he is less aggressive or speaks more softly than the others.

Encouraging Self-Diagnosis

The beauty of the Rocket technique is that it encourages youngsters to make the connection between the specific skills and the goals of interaction that they perceive as worth achieving. When they focus on the fifteen-second limit for expressing a thought, they can clearly see the value of learning to speak concisely despite the frustration of having to stay within that limit. If others give evidence that they are listening, then the compulsion to repeat what one says, to reword it anxiously for fear that the others will not hear it, loses its strength. And the relationship between each skill and its consequences is so clear that even the first-grader can appreciate it.

Such awareness of self, such appreciation of the needed skills, can also significantly change the pattern of pupil-teacher interaction. It becomes less necessary for the teacher to keep reminding and admonishing the student to "listen," "pay attention to what others are saying," "don't speak when someone else is speaking," "give someone else a chance to speak," and so on. The pattern of pupil interaction is regulated by the pupils themselves, and external controls become unnecessary.

Often the teacher feels, especially with very young children, that she had better do the observing in the Pre-Test and Post-Test. She feels that kindergartners are not equipped to observe the pattern of interaction, much less to record what they observe. Other teachers act as time-keepers during the four stages, because "My first-graders can't tell time," or "My seniors cannot be relied upon to take this seriously enough to keep accurate time." The teacher misses an excellent opportunity to help the pupils look at themselves and decide what they need, and also assume the responsibility for their own learning. As long as they must look to the teacher to tell them what they need, they will not learn how to diagnose their own needs adequately. The time will come when they will consciously feel the need for self-determination. When that time comes, they may respond chaotically and ineffectively because they have never learned the necessary skills.

There is also something to be said for self-diagnosis in its relation to motivation. When a group of young people says, "We certainly don't know how to do this, and our lack of skill results in ignoring some people, or in not getting the good out of a discussion," then they can decide more gracefully to practice that skill. If it is the teacher who points out the skill deficiency, then he must begin to plan how to motivate the pupils to accept his diagnosis as well as his remedy.

The kindergarten child can observe quite well during the Pre-Test if he is coached to observe only one thing, like whether or not the participants interrupt each other. Instead of having one observer, then, two or three children may act as observers, with each one looking for one aspect of interaction. The first-grader can use an egg-timer to keep time or gauge a time interval by how long it takes to put ten blocks into a box. And the high school seniors must not be diagnosed as irresponsible before they are given a chance to assume some responsibility in this situation.

Changing the Traditional Pattern of Classroom Management

The Rocket technique gives students and teachers some practice in changing the structure of the class. Just as the Affective Discussion cannot be conducted with the students seated in rows facing the teacher at the front of the room, so the Rocket needs a completely different arrangement from the traditional one. Because the goals in the Rocket are close at hand and clearly perceived by the pupils, and there is a specific structure necessary for reaching those goals, the technique provides an intermediate step between the traditional set-up and the open classroom.

Both the nature of the technique and the skills that the pupils learn contribute to the opening up of the classroom. One of the complaints about the open classroom, where pupils work individually and in small groups, is that it is too noisy. The Rocket skills contribute toward the solution of this problem. Children learn to speak one at a time, and this, alone, is enough to reduce the noise volume significantly in any group.

The open classroom requires that students work without constant teacher control and intervention. The Rocket, during which youngsters diagnose and time themselves, gives them a feeling of working without constant direction from above.

The open classroom requires that pupils work together at many tasks, that they treat each other with consideration in the use of materials and the acceptance of ideas. The Rocket helps them begin to see that there is more to getting together than just saying what you have to say.

All this is not to say that the use of the Rocket inevitably leads to change in classroom management. Not at all. However, it often serves to convince teachers that further relaxation of authoritarian control is worth trying, and to convince students that they have a unique contribution to make to their own education.

Avoiding the Pitfalls

Launching the Rocket

Questions for the Rocket may be taken from the responses on the Problem Census. It is necessary, however, to select those responses which do not have much affect. Since we are dealing here with affective topics, the tendency will be for teachers to use an emotional question to practice the stages of the Rocket. Actually, a very emotional topic should never be used as a vehicle for practicing a skill. The frustrations of dealing with strong emotions while, at the same time, being confronted with the frustrations of learning new skills are just too much to handle at once. Most children will just give up on the skills under the pressure of the need to express strong feelings and listen to the feelings of others.

Thus, questions like, "How do you feel about Black people?" or "How do you think Ute people feel about whites?" or "How do you feel when your father lectures you about drugs?" are not suitable for the initiation of the Rocket stages. Better to start the Rocket with something like, "How do you think age affects a person's attitudes toward race?" or "What do you see as the relationship between the government attitude over the years toward alcohol and toward drugs?" or, for younger children, "Where did the different people in this country come from?" Though all these topics deal with areas that people are very emotional about, the specific questions lean more toward the cognitive, and so generally can be discussed calmly.

Just as in the Problem Census and the Affective Discussion, we must avoid initiating questions that, by their nature, exclude some children from participation. The questions that say something like, "What are the parts of the human body?" or "Name the Supreme Court decisions that set the Federal policy of school integration," inevitably are beyond some children at that point in time when they are asked. Since the essential purpose of the Rocket is to practice skills, it is not reasonable to prevent some children from practicing just by the subject of the discussion, when it is so easy to avoid this.

Sometimes the teacher may hit on a question that he thinks will generate great interest and sustained discussion. However, after the first stage or so, the discussion fizzles out, and the group just sits there silent, or, as is more likely, begins to gossip in twos and threes about more personal concerns. It becomes apparent to the teacher who is circulating around the room that the purposes of the lesson are being subverted. The thing to do is to switch the group to another question quickly, and continue the skill lesson.

The time to prepare for this is at the beginning. Instead of telling each group what to discuss, it is a good idea to list three or four topics on the board and tell each group to pick one for the exercise. If the one the group selects does not sustain interest, the group can merely go on to another one of the suggested topics.

What should *not* be done is to leave the choice of topic completely open. Generally, too much time would be consumed by a group of eight people trying to make a choice of one out of an infinite number of topics. Of course, if the group says, "Can we talk about . . . ?" and there seems to be general agreement on this, by all means let them go ahead, if the topic is not too emotional. As long as we keep in mind that the discussion topic is merely a vehicle for practicing the skills, the process of choosing the topic should be done as expeditiously as possible.

Skipping a Stage

Teachers, after experiencing this technique in a college class, sometimes conclude that they cannot use one or another of the stages with their pupils. They feel that the youngsters are not equipped to deal with the exercise for reasons of skill or maturity. Here again, teachers seem to be looking for something called "success." If they feel that their children would be unable to reflect each other's contributions, then they think that there is no point in letting them try that stage. The expectation is that they will not succeed in their attempts at reflection, and so the lesson will not be a good one.

I must reiterate that, if the children were skillful at reflecting each other's ideas and if they listened carefully enough to do this, then they would not *need* the Four-Stage Rocket! It is because they cannot do these things, and they need the chance to practice, that the Rocket device is used.

Adapting the Technique for Your Class

One teacher developed a point system for making the Rocket more like a game. The group was penalized one point for every second a person went over or under the fifteen-second limit. This meant adding a scorekeeper who took his instruction from the time-keeper.

Another teacher made a large cardboard replica of a rocket with detachable stages. The payload in the cone was good discussion, which was left after the stages had been detached one by one.

The feeling that all four stages at one sitting is too much for any group of youngsters has led many teachers to devote only one stage to a lesson. They generally do the Pre-Test first, and give the pupils a chance to discuss their own pattern of interaction. Then they go on to Stage 1, or any other stage that deals with a skill deficiency that was revealed in the Pre-Test. If an immediate connection can be made by the students between a deficiency and the particular stage, they will probably be more motivated to practice the skill required in that stage.

After five or ten minutes on the chosen stage, the class discusses the purpose of the stage, how they felt about doing it, what effect they think it had on their discussion and on their discussion skill. They may choose to practice this same stage on several other occasions before they begin to deal with the other stages. Or they may, in subsequent lessons, take each stage in order, and then start over again.

Following is an account by one teacher of how she planned to use the Rocket:

> In adapting the Four-Stage Rocket for use with my second-graders I would make each stage applicable to a specific discussion assigned for a given day. I would assign two or three observers to specific tasks such as:
>
> 1. Did everyone contribute?
> 2. Was what each speaker said related to the discussion?
> 3. Did anyone dominate?
> 4. Did anyone keep cutting in?
>
> I would not ask them to record their evaluation as I do not feel they have the skills to listen, evaluate and record all in a given time

limit. Perhaps later I would cut the number down to one observer using a checklist of the above mentioned items.

The time allotted for each discussion will be increased from five to ten minutes allowing twenty-five seconds for each child's contribution. I would maintain the three-second interval in Stages three and four and by the time we get to the fourth stage of the Rocket I would cut the discussion time back from ten to eight minutes.

In Stages three and four I would select two helpers to assist the timekeeper in helping children keep track of what they said and to determine whether a speaker's statement showed that he understood and accurately reflected what the previous speaker had said (When a group of us teachers tried the Rocket, we found that we often did not remember what we ourselves had said! Sometimes we thought we had said one thing when we had actually said something entirely different.)

After several discussions I would try to combine the Pre-Test, Stages 1 and 2 and the Post-Test into a single fifteen-minute discussion allowing three or four minutes for each phase. At another time I would combine Stages three and four in a fifteen-minute discussion. Finally I would include the Pre- and Post-Test with Stages three and four in a twenty-minute discussion. Each discussion would be conducted on a different day.

4

The Mirrors

Description of the Technique

These are simple exercises to be done with the whole class. Let the pupils sit in a large circle, so that everyone can see everyone else.

i. Give each child a small hand mirror and instruct him to look at himself in the mirror. Then say: "Say what you see in the mirror." (Give each child an opportunity to respond.)

2. Say to the children: "Tell one thing you see in the mirror that you like."

3. Instruct the children: "Look at the person next to you. Tell him something you like about what you see."

Throughout, give the children opportunity to say how they feel about the exercise, how they feel about saying such things about themselves, how they feel when someone says such things about them.

4. Tell the children: "List all the things you like about your-

self. Let the person next to you tell you all the things he likes about you. Discuss with your neighbors (or in small groups) how your own list compares with what the other person told you about yourself, without revealing anything you prefer not to reveal. Repeat the exercise with another person."

5. Tell the children: "Write, 'I am good to look at because. . . .' I will not collect your papers."

6. Take a snapshot of each child (or use the hand mirrors). Have them look at the snapshot (or in the mirror) and begin to discuss: "Someday I will be a . . . ."

7. Flash pictures on a screen. The people in the pictures may be engaged in a variety of life situations. They must be of all racial groups (though not necessarily all in the same picture.) Encourage a discussion of the situations and children's conceptions of them and of the races of the people pictured.

For exercises 1 and 2, the teacher walks around the outside of the circle and touches each pupil when it is his turn to speak. The teacher says nothing, merely nods or smiles acceptance of each response and goes on to the next person quickly. No pupil should be urged to respond. The firm touch on the shoulder seems to make most people feel somewhat more comfortable about responding. However, should a pupil refuse to respond or say something that indicates reluctance, the teacher should make the same gesture of acceptance, and go on to the next person. Occasionally it may be necessary to say, "I don't think the people over there can hear you."

When the children are engaged in exercise 3, the teacher is not to listen in on the conversations. Permit those who wish it to move off into corners of the room for more privacy.

Throughout these exercises, the teacher maintains an air of acceptance and good humor so that the initial discomfort experienced by the children is not converted into hostility against the teacher or each other. However, there should be an obvious base of seriousness underlying the good humor, so that the children's discomfort does not result in an atmosphere of frivolousness and hilarity.

Rationale for Use of the Mirrors

Why Emphasize the Physical?

Often, when I do this technique with a group of teachers, they protest at my insistence that they talk about physical characteristics that they like about themselves and others. They insist that the nonphysical attributes of people are the important ones and that "Looks don't matter." This is the kind of platitude we have learned to articulate in our society. We present it as part of morality, as we do *Brotherhood* and *Love Your Neighbor*, but we don't really believe it! We are surrounded by evidence that the physical is very important to us indeed. Beauty contests are part of our culture; our actors and actresses (our twentieth-century folk heroes) are loved for their physical appearance; at the school dances the "plain" girls are not asked to dance; and plastic surgeons amass wealth from "nose jobs" and "face lifts," and rationalize what they do by defining some kind of universal need for beauty.

The fact is, the size and shape of a person's nose does matter to us, even though we maintain that, once we get to know a person, we never think of his looks. Never? Well, perhaps only those times when we introduce him to someone new. Or perhaps only those times when we notice people staring (or avoiding staring) in public.

No matter what philosophy we subscribe to about the relative importance of the spiritual as opposed to the material, psychologically we must come to terms with our physical being if we are to function adequately. Whatever else we are, we are also physical. If we cannot accept our physical self—see it, appreciate its beauty, like it—then we live emotionally handicapped. We doubt that we are beautiful and we conclude that we do not have a full measure of worth.

This concept is reduced almost to horrible absurdity by the teacher who proudly maintained that she never mentioned the fact that one of the children in her class had only one arm. "Nobody ever mentioned it?" I asked her. "Certainly not. I wouldn't let anybody talk about it. It didn't matter that he had one arm; he had many other characteristics that were more important."

Here was a child with only a left arm, living in a society where people used their right hands to greet each other, and *it didn't matter enough to talk about!* Here was a child who was never picked by the other children to be on a ball team, but nobody ever talked about it in class. Here was a child who, when he got into altercations with other children, was taunted about having only one arm, but the teacher quickly silenced these taunts—as soon as she heard them!

It wasn't important that he had only one arm? Important to *whom*, for pity's sake! The child was made to feel different. He was insulted and rejected. He had all kinds of feelings about it—anger, sadness, self-doubt—but he had to keep them to himself, at least in class. It certainly *was* important to the other children, and its importance was intensified by the air of secrecy and anxiety engendered by the teacher's ban on talking about it.

What the teacher was saying, of course, was that people should not be accepted or rejected on the basis of physical characteristics. What she was teaching the children was that she preferred to pretend that physical differences did not exist. Also, she communicated very clearly that there are some physical characteristics that should not be mentioned.

A Realistic Self-Concept and Success in School

The way children picture themselves affects their behavior. When children see themselves as inadequate, unlikeable, or unworthy, they often respond with lack of motivation to learn. They may demonstrate a lack of self-confidence or they may be talkative. Many of us who have worked with children have had this experience: we explain the mathematical process for solving a problem, and then we ask one of the children to replicate the process. We know, with every teaching instinct we have, that this child is quite capable of going through the process. But, "I can't," he says. "I can't do it." And he will not even take the chalk in his hand. "I'll help you," we say. "What's the first number?" He puts his clenched fists behind his back and tightens his jaw, firmly convinced that he will never be able to do it. This child is so sure he will fail that he cannot even try. He pictures himself as a failure, and so all his behavior is unconsciously designed to be consistent with this picture. To say he lacks self-confidence is too simple a diagnosis. He actually is impelled to cause his own failure because he cannot imagine himself a success.

Similarly, the child who feels that he is not a worthwhile person or a person that others can like will perceive himself as not worth succeeding. Since learning in school is generally recognized as success, he will feel unable to make the effort or take the steps to learn. Pointing out to this child that if he does not do his assignments he will never succeed in the world, will not motivate him to learn. On the contrary, it will merely reinforce his failing behavior.

The pupil who constantly talks in class is also setting himself up for failure in school. He is inevitably labeled a discipline problem, and teachers give up on trying to teach him. His talking is saying something important to anyone who will listen: "Please, see me. Hear me. Am I really so unworthy? Look at me. Reassure me." But the reassurance is not forthcoming. Only the reprimands, the expressions of annoyance, the rejection, all of which reinforce his feelings of unworthiness.

Our personal feelings of annoyance and rejection apart, no child is inherently unworthy. If some of us dislike him, there are others who, if they knew him, would like him very much. A person is inadequate only if the demands made on him violate *him* in some way: anticipate his readiness, ignore his previous experiences, impose on him alien standards. Realistically, then, each person is worthy of acceptance. Each person is worth teaching; each person is entitled to see himself as likeable and capable of succeeding. And, unless we can help children to see themselves thus, realistically, they will have severe impediments to success in school.

Overcoming the Destructive Effects of Racism

Minority-group children infer much from the total society about their inferiority. The adults in their lives are systematically excluded from many types of jobs. Around the dinner table, they hear stories of discrimination, often told by adults who are discouraged and defeated. Teachers often imply that they are inherently deficient in one way or another. If the mass media are beginning to depict them in less stereotyped ways, they are still living with parents and older brothers and sisters who saw themselves pictured as mentally and physically inferior. Can we honestly convince a Black child that skin color "doesn't matter?" He knows very well that skin color is a significant factor in the lives of us all.

School has never effectively intervened to teach the Black child, the Indian child, the Mexican, the Puerto Rican, that he is *not* inferior. School has not helped him see that, if people are prejudiced against him, this is *their* deficiency, not his, and that there is nothing wrong with him! The exercises with the mirrors help children to say loudly and clearly, "Black is beautiful!" or "Brown is beautiful!"

The self-concepts of majority children, too, are damaged by what they infer from the total society about their superiority. From the day they begin to watch television, it becomes clear that Black people, brown people and those who speak with accents are not the most important people in our world. Saturday morning children's shows make it abundantly clear that Orientals are villains and that an accent identifies the despot. In school most children are learning from books that do not even suggest that there are people in the United States who are not white, except the Indians who still dry meats for preserving and live in tepees.

Not only are white children kept in ignorance of what other groups must live with in our society, but they absorb the idea that they are somehow superior for being white. This is a concept of self that is at least as unrealistic as the Black child's self-concept of inferiority, and can result in severe disadvantages in the course of his life. For example, his belief that just because he is white he will automatically get job preference is no longer completely true. In open competition with qualified applicants of all races, he will have to rely on more than just his whiteness for success. If he doesn't get the job he thinks is due him, the disappointment may cause him to give up. He may rationalize his continuing failure by saying it's no use, he doesn't have a chance in this world he never knew. He may even begin to believe that there is something about his being white that caused his failure, and, since there is no help for whiteness, he is forever at a disadvantage.

There are some white people who, knowing something about what white society has done to Black people, and feeling powerless to make amends, develop feelings of guilt about being white. I have met young white students who want to be teachers of poor Black youngsters and who are severely handicapped in their effectiveness because of their feelings of guilt. Their relief at being white conflicts with their need to deny their whiteness and their resulting behavior does little good for the child they teach. They sometimes cry a little over him, they are reluctant to make demands on him.

They present themselves almost as Black, really knowing the Black experience in America, and then they feel terribly defeated when the child and his parents continue to see him as white. Other white people have turned their anger against the victims of prejudice and discrimination, unconsciously seeing them as the cause of their own intolerable feelings of guilt.

Reducing the Need for Prejudice

The white person who knows who he is and accepts himself has a better chance of avoiding the pitfall of corrosive prejudice. On the one hand, he need not turn his feelings of guilt against the people who seem to be causing it. On the other, he need not look for scapegoats on whom to pin his own inadequacies. He will see himself as a person who has strengths as well as weaknesses, as we all have. And he will be able to accept this. He will not feel compelled to find whole groups of people who are "inferior" to him, so that he can see himself as comparatively superior.

Encouraging Group Cohesiveness

One big advantage of these exercises is that they are done in a large group, yet they do not contribute to the isolation of the individual pupil, as does most large-group class work. Usually, pupils in a class of thirty or forty recite to the teacher and are individually evaluated as correct or incorrect, whether they do their reciting orally or in writing. A "class discussion" also is, in effect, merely a recitation by a few of the most articulate and knowledgeable pupils.

Here, people begin to look at each other and at themselves in a somewhat different light. They begin to explore the values and attitudes of a society which has produced in all of them a reluctance to look at themselves and express open approval, or to look at each other and do the same. How interesting it is that we are not faulted when we look in a mirror in public and say "Oh, how *awful* I look!" And the teacher will find that, in the first exercise, many pupils will say something denigrating about themselves. At the very least, they will see only eyeglasses or a hair ribbon. And then with what difficulty they struggle with the instruction that they say something they like! What a sad commentary on our social values: commendation for denigrating one's self, and condemnation for approval of one's self! We even have words for it: vanity, conceit, swell-head. The children may begin to see that as a group they have much in common, even more important than their differences in academic achievement.

After a while, when they can comfortably see themselves in positive, accepting ways, and they feel safe enough to see each other the same way, the need for bickering and fighting among them is reduced. They can differ with each other without rejecting each other. They can openly appreciate and profit from each other's strengths, and accept with tolerance each other's deficiencies.

Self-Concept and Drug Use

There is ample clinical evidence that people who become addicted to drugs and alcohol generally suffer from low self-concepts. It is not so clear, however, whether they start with low self-concepts and are therefore drawn to drugs as a way of coping, or that becoming involved in drug use impairs their conceptions of themselves. Whatever the case, there is little doubt that there is a definite relationship between overuse of drugs (including alcohol) and low self-concept. The systematic intervention in education to get all children to see themselves realistically and positively may be part of the answer in helping them reject the use of drugs as crutches for getting through life. If, consciously, they accept themselves and see themselves as worthwhile, they will not seek unconsciousness (or, as some would have it, "heightened consciousness") in order to escape from what they are. Of course, the need to escape from the terrible realities of the world of the poor and the rejected is not dealt with by self-acceptance. But those who feel themselves worthwhile can consider alternatives to escape, and can begin to develop skills for changing the world. These are legitimate educational processes that can begin as soon as the child enters school.

Self-Concept and Relationships Between the Sexes

Early in children's lives, we begin to condition them to our social pattern of interaction between the sexes. Every teacher of sixth-graders has heard or advanced the observation that the boys are girls are "naturally" antagonistic toward each other. The solutions have been to keep them separate, and to encourage them to compete against each other. So girls are permitted to get their coats from the closet first, and to walk out at dismissal time unmolested by the boys. The boys must wait in their seats, impatiently shuffling their feet, until the girls are out of the building. (What happens outside the building is not the teacher's responsibility!) It is conceded that boys and girls must learn something about procreation—not sex, but reproduction—but they must do so apart from each other. The suggestion that these matters are something that concerns them both together and about which they must learn to communicate, meets with all manner of resistance, from shocked surprise to a shrugging denial that it can be seriously considered.

One argument by teachers against making sex education an opportunity to help children develop healthy conceptions of themselves and each other, is that parents would object. I have always found it interesting to listen to those same teachers who discuss the need for educating parents to the values of the curriculum (especially poor parents!) abandon all thought of educating parents to the values of sex education. If half the zeal that goes into spreading the dogma of the new math were put into convincing the community of the importance of teaching boys and girls to talk to each other and appreciate each other as whole human beings, we might have fewer divorces and far fewer precipitous marriages. However, we observe the tension between them that is clearly a function of growing heterosexual awareness, and it does nothing but disturb us.

So disturbed are we, that we actually set up roadblocks to any kind of communication, and encourage the children to see each other as competing opponents, in games, in academic achievement and in getting teacher approval for their nonacademic behavior. "They love competing with each other," is the argument. (Don't we always let the children do what they love to do in school?!)

It reminds me of an incident that occurred when I was teaching police recruits at the Police Academy some years ago. Walking across a drill field, I saw two groups of recruits facing each other. One group, all Black, held all kinds of miscellaneous objects, apparently for throwing—stones, garbage can lids, and so on. The opposing group, all white, carried the broom handles they used for practice rifles. Under the direction of the sergeant, they were squaring off to attack each other, in some bizarre simulation of a riot. When I asked the sergeant why he had separated the Blacks and whites and squared them off against each other, he explained that he was using the natural antagonism between the two groups to produce some enthusiastic participation in their training. This, in a department and in a city where prejudice and discrimination against Black people was shortly to explode into bloodshed!

The need to see women as inferior or inadequate, or the need to see men as competitors is at least partly a function of the individual's conception of his own adequacy and worth. The self-actualizing individual, comfortable with reality, accepting of himself and others, democratically oriented and concerned with helping people, has no need to find the level of his worth by perceiving others as inferior—neither other races, nor the other sex. On the contrary, he sees the differences between his own and other groups as functional and valuable. Boys and girls must see themselves and each other as whole human beings, rather than as one-dimensional sex symbols. The competent engineer is just that: a competent engineer, whether a man or woman. The difference between the two is that the woman bears a child. Beyond that, her sex is immaterial. If children perceive sex differences as indications of inferiority or superiority, perhaps it is because, unable to accept themselves as valuable, they cannot afford to accept others as valuable.

Self-Concept and Relationships with Adults

It is not difficult for children to come away from their relationships with adults feeling inadequate and inferior. They hear much from adults about their errors and misbehaviors. What is it an adult usually asks a small child he hasn't seen for several hours? "Were you a good boy today?" he asks. The implication is clear: "Come on, confess. What did you do that you shouldn't have done?"

Even as teachers, how many of us adults return written assignments to children with all the *correct* answers marked in red? Very few, I think. There is a difference between getting a paper that prompts one to say, "Oh, look at all I got wrong!" and getting a paper on which the markings move one to rejoice, "Look at all I got right!"

I know a mathematics teacher who teaches this way. "Surely," you may say, "a math problem is correct or incorrect. And it is no favor to the child to tell him he is doing the math correctly when he is not." But this teacher, sitting on the floor of the classroom with a gaggle of fourth-graders around her, rejoices when a child gives an answer, "You're almost right!" And the child smiles and bends his head over the slate to try again.

It's really a matter of emphasis. Do we emphasize the positive, the successes, or do we make a major point of the failures and say nothing about the successes? And do we justify this by maintaining that we are just trying to teach the child, change him for the better? By pointing out what he must change about himself, don't we help him to change, for the good of his own growth and maturation? It might be well for us to consider the evidence that the child who feels good about his successes is encouraged to keep going, while the child who hears too much about his failures can be persuaded to abandon further efforts to succeed.

As adults we must be careful not to displace our own feelings of anger and frustration on to the children who can be, in effect, our captive targets. Children who are continually glowered at, punished for minor or imagined transgressions, and generally given evidence that they are disliked, begin to feel that there is something really wrong with them, that they are somehow inherently unlikeable. Especially vulnerable are the children of teachers who feel that their efforts at teaching are not successful. Such a teacher, instead of being provided with the professional help she needs, may be additionally burdened down by the criticisms of the principal and the complaints of parents. Unable to live with the awareness of failure, this teacher displaces her own feelings of inadequacy on to the children.

Going Beyond the Technique

If we are really to see education as going beyond the objective of changing the student's perception of his environment, and to see it also as deliberately intervening to change the student's perception of himself, then obviously we must do more than the few simple exercises suggested here. The idea is to use the underlying rationale for the exercises as a basis for looking at everything we do in the classroom. For example, if it is agreed that children need to accept themselves as adequate and worthwhile, then we must do all we can to provide success experiences for them. Those who are most persistently failing are the very ones who most need success. Here the ingenuity and skill of the teacher must come into play, for she must first broaden her criteria for success in school, in such a way that it is clear to the pupils that she is not just making concessions to their disabilities. If skill in art or sensitivity to others' needs are really valued achievements in the classroom, then they must receive equal recognition with history and mathematics, both in the time spent on developing them and in the space given to them on report cards. We have all had experience with the class "dummy" who was so helpful at carrying books and was always complimented on this skill so that he too could have some success in school. But no one was fooled. The children saw him as the odd one, the one who at best needed their compassion. But he was never in the mainstream of their society, and more often was the butt of their hostilities. The child who is not achieving academically at that time in his life when he is with us needs to know that he is somebody worthwhile, even though it is taking him a long time to learn long division. And those who learn long division quickly need to know that this does not give them license to look down on others.

Just in passing, it might we well to note that people denied rewards in life tend to overemphasize status. Many of those whites who become violent when a Black family buys a house in the neighborhood are responding out of threat to their status. If Blacks whom they see as inferior can afford what they can afford, then how satisfied can they be with what they have achieved in life? The status that goes with being "popular" in school may be so sought after because other rewards are not forthcoming. And popularity often is achieved by getting into drugs, because that is what the crowd is doing. The status needs satisfied by membership in violent gangs may also be a function of failure in other aspects of life. Since, for a significant part of his life, the individual's main source of reward is school, it falls to the teacher to use a considerable portion of her professional energy and expertise to provide children with opportunities for successes that have meaning for them.

Not all success needs to be first-hand. Vicarious success experiences can also be valuable in developing positive, realistic self-concepts. Many such experiences may be found in the success of individuals with whom children can identify. Though we have often taught Black children about great Black historical figures, we have tended to rely a little too heavily on this for motivating children to succeed. Not infrequently, the historical figure is too remote, too much a giant, for the child to see himself in that role. We must look for vicarious experiences closer to home. (See Chapter 7 for some ideas on this.)

Above all, what the child needs if he is to perceive himself in positive, realistic terms is a sense of control over his environment and over his life. Children who succeed in school seem to have this. Other children feel powerless, at the mercy of chance and fate. This is really the theme that runs through this whole book: As teachers we need to help children grow into a conviction that they are capable of changing their lives, and making their world what they want it to be. Traditionally, we have tried to teach this by laying out a plan of action for the children (getting good grades, behaving properly, and so on) and engaging in some exhortation to keep them on course. This method has not worked well. Poor children continue to fail in school and middle-class children become disillusioned and cynical. Perhaps we can get better results with different approaches.

One thing we can do is deal accurately with history and contemporary life, giving adequate and honest consideration to all groups of people. Both majority and minority children can get a more realistic sense of their own place in the development of the world so that they can begin to concern themselves with their own role in the continuing course of this development. We cannot stop with teaching the past accurately; we must also deal with the present in realistic terms. If we do this, young people will clearly see the connection between school and the other parts of their lives, and know that the skills they develop in school are the ones they will need to control their destinies.

How Adults and Children Respond to the Technique

One teacher, asking her third-graders to say what they see in the mirror, was moved almost to tears by the class bully who looked at himself for a long while and then said, "Zero. I'm a big nothing. I don't count." Suddenly, she realized how all the reprimands delivered to him, all the punishments, all the times the other children rejected and excluded him contributed to this conception of himself, and contributed also to his continuing bullying and hostility.

Similarly, another child, a sixth-grader, quiet and withdrawn, responded, "I don't want to say anything because there is nothing important in the mirror." Still another, with a face as appealing as any seven-year-old's, turned away from the mirror with a grimace and said, "I don't want to see my ugly face."

On the other hand, one fourth-grader, after telling the child next to her what she liked about him, and hearing something similar from him in turn, almost shouted, "I feel like telling each one in the room what I like about them!"

Teachers often report that children of all ages do some giggling and squirming when the exercises are begun. But as one reports, "As time went on, there was less giggling and more interest of a serious nature evolved." I have had similar experiences with adults who felt very uncomfortable at the outset, but warmed to the idea and changed from an attitude of wariness and reluctance to give too much of themselves, to smiling, relaxed individuals, ready to give and take in friendly fashion.

Very often, people who have worked together for years are most reluctant to say something "I like" about each other. One man insisted he couldn't think of anything special to say, "and anyhow she knows how I feel." It was not until several sessions later that "she" announced that he had never indicated any appreciation of her work and she often felt depressed about this.

A twelfth-grader said, "I like to hear what people like about me," and a third-grader thought aloud, musingly, "When we talk about what we like we can stop gang wars."

One teacher thought she had learned something significant about the self-concepts of a group of poor Black children when she wrote: "I asked the children what they would like to do when they grew up and I got answers like, 'Be a fireman?' 'Be a nurse?' 'Work in a bar?' All with a question mark."

One principal, after being exposed to the technique, wrote, "During a recent staff meeting I suggested that it was necessary for teachers to devise classroom activities that would enable children to develop positive feelings about themselves. As the discussion progressed, it became evident that, though they were in accord with the need to help others, they resisted the idea that we all need to look at ourselves." He, as have other people I have done this with, had become convinced that self-awareness is a key factor in developing a positive, realistic concept of self.

He and others have devised many games and exercises designed to help themselves and their colleagues grow to self-awareness: One principal asked his teachers to think of the pattern of their lives and draw "life-style maps," picturing the relative sizes, shapes and directions of the various facets of their lives. Another asked teachers in a group to think of a word or phrase that best described each person in the group. In the process of sharing these words, each participant drew a multi-faceted idea of how his colleagues pictured him. Later, they discussed how the group concepts compared to their self-concepts.

But the point of these self-concept exercises is made quite clear in the words of one seven-year-old whose teacher had spent two months carrying out an intensive plan to help her children develop positive self-concepts. Using one exercise as a check on progress at the end of that period, she got this response: "I am good to look at because I'm good looking and plus I like my hair and my ears and I like my legs and I like my stomach and I like my shoes and plus I like my whole body."

5

Role-Playing*

Description of the Technique

The Steps in Role-Playing

Step 1: Telling the Story   First the teacher must present the situation for role-playing to the class. The situation may be taken from an incident that happened and that the children know about, or it may be one that the teacher has made up, using elements that are to be found in the experiences of the children. Often, the teacher will use a situation that he feels the children may experience in the future, with an eye to preparing them to deal with similar situations after they leave school.

The teacher reads the situation to the class, making sure—at least when she first uses the technique—that the characters all have names and that the problem is clearly delineated. At first the problems should be relatively simple to stage-manage, involving two to

*A brief overview of the objectives of role-playing in the classroom appears in Epstein, *Intergroup Relations for the Classroom Teacher* (Boston: Houghton Mifflin Co., 1968) pp. 107–9.

five people. Even if the situation is taken from an an experience that the children have recently had, it is better to tell it like a story, so that the children are encouraged to approach it with objectivity, uncommitted to justifying what they did in the real situation. Certainly the role-names should be fictitious.

The reading of the incident should end after one of the characters has said or done something decisive, so that the class is naturally moved to pick up the story at that point and move it forward. When the reading ends, the teacher says, "Now what happens?" or "How do you think Alice felt?" These questions encourage the class to imagine ways in which the story may continue, and to put themselves in the shoes of one or another of the characters.

The teacher must be careful that the discussion does not go on for long and that individuals do not elaborate on the endings they propose. The danger is that the discussion may become a substitute for the role-playing, with alternative solutions suggested and rejected verbally, and the role-playing becoming only an anti-climax. Should a pupil begin to elaborate, the teacher merely suggests that, instead of talking about it, he take one of the roles and "show us" how it happens.

Step 2: Casting the Roles   The idea is to select as role-players those people who have some feeling for the characters or some idea of how the story might proceed. This is one of the times when the teacher does *not* ask: "Who would like to play the roles?" Especially with older pupils, or with adults, there is a strong possibility that no one will feel comfortable enough to volunteer. People are afraid to get up and "act" in front of their peers, especially when they have never participated in role-playing before. A call for volunteers may result in the end of the lesson before it begins.

Nor should the teacher say to a student, tentatively and softly, "Would you like to be Mr. Smith?" The student may say with a shudder "No, not me." The teacher then must go to another student and ask, "Would *you* like to be Mr. Smith?" Again the response may be "No." Well, one may as well give up the idea of role-playing for that day, because it is the rare pupil who will say yes after two or three of his classmates have said no.

When the story is read and a very short discussion has followed, the teacher then says firmly to those pupils he has identified as having some feeling for the situation, "You play Mr. Smith, you be

Mr. Jones." He does this expeditiously, smiling calmly in the face of some shivers of apprehensions and expressions of doubt.

Step 3: Involving the Whole Class   When all the characters have been picked, the teacher asks them to leave the room, or retire to one corner of the room and chat quietly for a few minutes among themselves. They are not supposed to be planning the role-playing or discussing it, unless they happen to want to. The idea is for them to be otherwise occupied while the teacher works with the rest of the class.

The teacher asks the class, "What shall we look for as the scene unfolds?" And she writes the various suggestions on a sheet of experience chart paper. No matter what the age of the group is, she will get responses like: How will they solve the problem? Will somebody get angry? How will the other characters respond to the anger? Will the characters take sides?

When all the responses are written on the chart paper, she asks pupils to watch and report on each one after the role-playing. Those pupils who are not assigned to watch for a specific response are to watch for any unexpected developments. Everyone is encouraged to take notes of his observations, because it is easy to forget important items. The teacher also takes notes so that she may have material for leading the discussion.

This step is important because it makes participants of the whole class. It takes them out of the role of audience, as it takes the role-playing out of the realm of an entertainment. This discourages them from later discussing whether the "acting" is good or bad. The class is reminded that role-playing is not an easy thing to do, that they should not laugh at or make comments to the role-players, but should concentrate on looking for the various aspects of the interaction so that they may be discussed afterwards.

The chart with the list of items is then reversed so the role-players are not influenced by what the class is looking for.

Step 4: Role-playing the Situation   The role-players are called in and told to take up the scene where the story ended. They may pull up a chair or two as props, but the teacher should refrain from "stage-managing the production." If the role-players question her about how to start, she is to say, "Do it any way you like." There may be a moment or two of confusion, but it is better for the players to make the decisions about how to proceed, than for the teacher to influence the outcome by imposing her decisions.

The scene is played until there is enough material presented for analysis and discussion. Sometimes the players themselves stop, when they feel they have gone as far as they can with it. Sometimes the teacher may stop the scene, when the players are beginning to repeat themselves in their attempts at solution.

The teacher must refrain from stopping the scene because the voices are getting loud or the action is picking up. If role-playing is to be valuable as an opportunity for solving real problems, then it must simulate reality as closely as possible. I would step in to prevent a blow from landing, but it would be a grave mistake to intervene because the players are "getting excited" and may possibly "lose control." I must note that in hundreds of role-playing situations with youngsters and adults, my students and I have never had anyone strike anyone else.

Sometimes, in the course of the role-playing, one of the players steps out of character to "explain" what he is doing or what he intends to do. This must be discouraged. The teacher must say, "Just do it. Go on with the scene."

Step 5: Reinforcing the Feeling of Safety   When the role-playing is over, the teacher asks each player, "How did you feel doing this?" This is an opportunity for the player to protect himself from any perceived threat. For example, he may, in the course of the role-playing, have said something that he is afraid will be misconstrued by his classmates. Or he may have revealed more about his own attitudes than he now thinks politic. This is the time when he can say, "When I said that, I was only role-playing; that's not how I really feel." or "I really didn't feel anything; all this isn't real to me."

The teacher just accepts each response without comment. However, she must cut short any long comment on the whole role-playing situation. She may say, "We'll discuss all that in a moment. For now just tell us how you felt."

Step 6: Discussing the Observations   Now the class talks about what it observed and begins to evaluate the solutions presented. Throughout the discussion, the teacher may need to remind the pupils to refer to the players by their *role* names, not their real names. This makes it clear that the discussion refers to the characters in the situation, not to classmates. Thus, comments and criticisms need not be taken personally nor actions defended in the same way. The focus can remain on the problem presented.

Step 7: Trying Alternative Solutions   As the discussion proceeds, people begin to suggest other ways of solving the problem. Or they maintain that if somebody had done something differently, the outcome would have been different. The teacher asks those individuals who make such suggestions to try them out by role-playing.

Sometimes, all the roles are taken by new people. Sometimes, the only new people are the ones who suggested different behaviors. The new play may be taken up at any point, depending on what the players want to demonstrate.

Again, after the role-playing the class discusses the efficacy of the solution and perhaps someone sees another possibility. In this case, the scene is played again—and again—as many times as the class wants to.

Step 8: Sharing Data and Making Conclusions   At some point the pupils begin to compare the various solutions, and to bring into the discussion additional data from their own experiences. They may come to some general conclusions about similar situations. Or they may decide that no satisfactory solution was presented. In this case they may conclude (or the teacher may suggest) that additional information or further experiences may be needed before other solutions are explored. Pupils and teachers then begin to plan for these experiences.

A Role-Playing Session

The class is made up of Black, Puerto Rican and mainland white students, tenth-graders in a school somewhat west of the central core of a large eastern city.

TEACHER: Last week, when we did a problem census on what you wanted to know about race, one of you said, "Integration is fine in elementary school, but it causes too many problems in high school." Today I have a story about some high school students. Let me read it to you:

Linda is an attractive tenth-grade student. She is white. She is popular with her classmates. José is a Puerto

Rican student. He is a handsome young man, with brown skin and tightly curled black hair. He also is a good student and has recently been elected to the Student Council. He and Linda have become very friendly. Finally one day he asks her to go to the movies with him. She really wants to go, but even as she thinks this she feels uncomfortable—almost afraid. But she says yes. When Linda tells her mother about the date she has made with José, her mother becomes very flustered and says, "But he is not our kind."

CLASS: *(Silence)*

JIM: What's Linda afraid of?

AMY: I know how she feels. What will people say?

GEORGE: My father doesn't want me going out with people who aren't Puerto Rican.

SUSAN: Her mother will get all upset and then she'll have to make up some story. If I were Linda . . .

TEACHER: *(Interrupting)* Wait. Instead of just talking about what might happen, why don't we *let* it happen right here, where we can see it? Amy, you be Linda.

AMY: Oh—oh . . .

TEACHER: *(Smiling)* George, you be Amy's father. We'll change the mother in the story to the father.

CLASS: *(Laughter)*

TEACHER: George and Amy, would you step out in the hall for a couple of minutes while we talk in here? You don't have to discuss the story unless you want to. *(They leave.)* Now, as they act out the story, what are some of the things we can watch for?

SUSAN: Let's see what she does when her father gets upset.

TEACHER: *(Writes response on chart paper.)* What else can we watch for?

WILLIAM: Maybe her father won't get upset.

JANE: He'll call her mother.

WILLIAM: No he won't.

TEACHER: *(Writes "See if father calls in mother.")*

JIM: See if Linda can convince her father.

TEACHER:	*(Writes response.)*
BEVERLY:	Do they both get mad and walk out?
TEACHER:	*(Writes response.)*
BARBARA:	Look for facial expressions. Sometimes people say one thing but really *feel* like saying the opposite.
TEACHER:	*(Writes "Look for facial expressions.")* Anything else? *(Silence.)*
TEACHER:	All right. Now, who will watch for what Linda does when her father gets upset?
SUSAN:	*(Raises hand.)*
TEACHER:	Who will make a note of the father's behavior if he doesn't get upset.
WILLIAM:	*(Raises hand.)*
TEACHER:	Who'll see if he calls in the mother?
JANE and WILLIAM:	I will.
TEACHER:	All right. Both of you do that. Who'll watch and see what Linda does to try to convince her father?
JIM:	*(Raises hand.)*
TEACHER:	Who will see if they both get mad—or what they feel?
CLASS:	*(No response.)*
TEACHER:	Come on, Beverly, weren't you interested in this one?
CLASS:	*(Laughter)*
BEVERLY:	O.K. I'll watch.
TEACHER:	Facial expressions—who'll make a note of those? Barbara?
ELLEN:	I'd like to.
TEACHER:	All right, Ellen. Barbara, you do that too if you want to.
	Everyone else watch for any of these things or for anything unexpected that may happen. I think you'll find that you have to take notes on your observations, or you'll forget some of them. *(Turns the chart to the wall.)*
	Let's get the players in now and see what happens. But before we do, remember, getting up in front of the room and acting is not easy. So no laughing or telling the players what to do. It interferes with the scene.

George and Amy come in and stand in front of the room, obviously uncertain about what is expected of them.

TEACHER: Remember, Amy's father says, "He's not our kind." Pick it up from there. *(Teacher sits with class.)*

AMY: Do we sit down?

GEORGE: I'll be sitting in my easy chair. (Pulls up a chair and sits down.)

AMY: O.K. I'll be standing.

CLASS: *(Some giggles heard)*

TEACHER: Sh—sh—. *(To players)* Go ahead.

AMY: Dad, I want to talk to you.

GEORGE: Yes, Amy?

TEACHER: Linda—that's Linda.

GEORGE: Yes, Linda?

AMY: I don't know how you'll feel about this. But José asked me to go to the movies with him.

GEORGE: You have homework to do!

AMY: This is for Saturday night, Dad!

GEORGE: Well, I don't think your mother will like the idea.

AMY: Why not? José is a very nice boy. He's on the Student Council and everything.

GEORGE: Aren't there any other nice boys in school? What about William?

CLASS: *(Laughter)*

AMY: José asked me to go and I'm going! You never let me do anything! Other fathers want their daughters to be popular! You're always telling me not to do something! Well, I'm going to the movies with José! I am! I am! *(She turns and runs to the side of the room, as if she were running out.)*

TEACHER: Can we stop now and look at what happened? Linda, come back and sit down in front so we can talk to you. You both did very well! Now, Dad, how did you feel in this situation?

GEORGE: I didn't feel anything.

TEACHER:	All right. Linda, how did you feel?
LINDA:	That's what happens. I could just feel myself getting angry, even though it was just a play.
TEACHER:	All right. Let's have some of the results of our observations. *(Turns chart to show the items to be observed.)*
JANE:	He didn't call her mother—though he tried to put it off on her.
WILLIAM:	If it had gone on a little longer he would have called her. My father always . . .
TEACHER:	Let's stay with what happened here for now.
BARBARA:	Did you see the look on George's face?
TEACHER:	The *father's* face, Barbara.
BARBARA:	The father's face. He was scared too.
GEORGE:	I was expecting this. It was bound to happen with all those different people going to the same school.
BEVERLY:	Linda didn't really do any good. Running out mad doesn't solve the problem. Her father just won't let her go.
WILLIAM:	Maybe it would have been better if her father did get angry and say what he really thought.
TEACHER:	Well, why don't we try it again. Beverly, you be Linda this time and . . .
WILLIAM:	Let me be the father.
TEACHER:	All right. Let's try it again.
BEVERLY:	Dad, José asked me to go to the movies with him this weekend.
WILLIAM:	How does your mother feel about this?
CLASS:	*(Laughter)*
WILLIAM:	I mean—why do you want to go with him?
BEVERLY:	I like him. He's a good friend.
WILLIAM:	People should stay with their own kind.
BEVERLY:	He's a very nice boy, Dad. What do you have against him?
WILLIAM:	I don't have anything against him. It's just that he's Puerto Rican.
BEVERLY:	What's wrong with that? Don't you always tell me that

it's the kind of person you are that's important, not your religion or anything?

WILLIAM: Yes, but—

BEVERLY: Didn't you mean it when you said it?

WILLIAM: Well, why don't we talk about it after dinner?

BEVERLY: Oh—all right.

TEACHER: That was fine. Now, Dad, how did you feel about this?

WILLIAM: I felt sort of stuck. I didn't know how to get out of it.

BEVERLY: I think I had him there. Now all I have to do is convince my mother.

JOHN: I think he'll have to let her go now, or he'll look like a phony.

RITA: He'll find some way to get out of it.

JOHN: I don't think so. He may not like it that she's going with a Puerto Rican, but he won't be able to do anything about it.

ELIZABETH: Maybe when he meets José and sees how nice he is, he'll say it's O.K.

HARRY: Didn't José have brown skin? When he meets him, he'll *really* stop it.

CLASS: *(Laughter)*

JOHN: That's true. As soon as you get into different races, then there's real trouble.

RITA: What do you mean? Why should there be trouble. In my family there are people with all colors skin. It doesn't make any difference.

HARRY: My great-grandfather was an Indian.

CLASS: *(Catcalls and laughter.)*

WILLIAM: Maybe it's true—maybe people of different races shouldn't get serious about each other. If they get married, the children suffer.

BEVERLY: How do you know? You just heard someone say that.
     (The bell rings.)

TEACHER: That was great. Let's pick up our discussion again next time. Maybe we can get some more information on interracial dating and marriage.

Now the teacher's work begins: to diagnose the educational needs revealed during the lesson and to plan for learning experiences to provide for those needs. The teacher makes some notes:

1. The pupils certainly caught on to the role-playing quickly. They really did very well! They apparently enjoyed it, and they were able to get at some important insights.
2. There is an area of inner conflict in some of the boys and girls. They have been taught about valuing a person for his own qualities—and yet they have also been taught to limit their relationships with people of other groups. They need to clarify their own values. Also, the whole matter of interracial contact is disturbing to them. They need more time to talk about their feelings.
3. They need more simulated situations so they can practice developing communication skills with parents and other adults. There seems to be a strong feeling that there's no use trying to talk to parents.
4. They need more information about different groups and more vicarious experiences of intergroup contact, perhaps through literature.

Pitfalls to Avoid

Falling into a Pattern of "Disciplining" and Punitiveness

A role-playing session does not lend itself to the traditional pattern of classroom management, where the teacher expects silence, low-key application to note-taking or other writing, and complete reliance on the teacher's lead. As a matter of fact, the more familiar the pupils become with the technique, the more likely they are to want to use it as problems arise, the more involved they will get in each session, and, consequently the more emotion they will express both in the role-playing and in the sharing of observations and experiences.

Almost inevitably, there will be times when the talking gets loud, when people don't wait for the appropriate time to speak, and even times when people are moved to express themselves in very emotional language. It is a mistake for the teacher at these times to demand conformity to traditional classroom patterns on the threat of disciplinary action. As soon as the teacher gets into a quarrel with a student, the spontaneity and involvement that characterizes role-playing is lost, and the students once more are wary of stepping out of their classroom roles. Though the teacher must, at first, be firm in guiding her students through the steps of the technique if they are to achieve the objectives of role-playing, the firmness must be understood by them as related to the technique, and not to the maintenance of discipline.

Memorizing Lines or Planning in Advance

Role-playing is not the same as putting on a play. The insights gained are the result of spontaneous involvement in the roles rather than "learning a part." Children who have been attending school for some time seem to fall into the "presentation" syndrome. Every time they achieve a feeling of success at some thing, they want to "present" it in assembly or to other classes. Often, teachers are so delighted with their enthusiasm and involvement that they succumb to the children's urging.

Now, there is nothing wrong with children putting on an entertainment in the assembly if that is what they want to do. However, what they get out of a role-playing session can generally *not* be communicated to an audience. Especially after they have polished the dialogue and locked the scenes into a one- or two-act play, and picked the best actors, the essential purposes of role-playing are lost: free expression of feelings, the spontaneity, the groping for alternative solutions. Writing and presenting a play is an altogether different kind of activity.

Having a Nonparticipating Audience

Role-playing is for everyone who is in the room. People who are "just watching" or "observing" put the participants into an unfair position. While the participants are taking some risks in revealing their feelings and attitudes, in taking on roles, and in analyzing behaviors, the nonparticipants are maintaining absolute safety by giving nothing. It is relatively easy for them, from this perspective, to maintain a critical and even patronizing attitude that can communicate itself to the participants and make them self-conscious and resentful. Everyone in the room—including the teacher—should be prepared to participate actively. (It is not unusual for pupils to suggest that the teacher take a particular role. The teacher must be careful, however, not to permit the inference that his way of playing a role is the best way. It must be only *one* of the alternatives, and open to analysis and evaluation as are the other alternatives.)

Psyching Out the Players

One of the things to watch out for in role-playing is the tendency of many people of all ages to engage in psychological analysis of others. There is great temptation to attribute motives and feelings, not to the characters being played, but to the people playing them. The teacher cannot permit this to happen, because it makes role-playing too threatening an activity. People end up defensively trying to justify their own behaviors or angrily denying that they have been accurately analyzed. Or role-playing may turn into the kind of wrenching psychodrama that deals with problems on a level that should be attempted only by someone trained in psychology or psychiatry.

If the teacher insists that the discussion focus in on the *roles* rather than on real personalities and if she makes people refer to the characters by their role names at all times, she can usually maintain the role-playing at the level suitable for the classroom.

Rationale for the Technique

Real Problems Faced by the Pupils

Role-playing is used in a variety of ways to make learning more interesting. However, there is one reason for using role-playing in classrooms that, perhaps, most teachers have not considered. Youngsters encounter many life situations that frighten, puzzle and confuse them. A child is called "nigger" or "chink" by someone he considered a friend. He feels the hurt and the anger. Whatever he does about it, he does on the spur of the moment, and the consequences of his behavior strike him with the force of surprise and lack of preparedness.

A teenager is offered marijuana by several friends. They tease and cajole him when he hesitates to accept. All he brings to this moment are memories of the scare ads on TV and the exhortations of parents and other adults.

A sixth-grader begins to wonder about her relationship with boys. Somehow, the whispering, giggling sessions with her girlfriends do not answer the questions in her mind. Her mother gives information that does not apply, and her mother's obvious discomfort discourages the child from continuing the discussion.

How is the young person to deal productively with such situations and dozens of similar ones? Generally, the only preparation he has is lectures on morality, silence, or the confusing results of his observation of adult behavior. Just the other day, a mother and her four-year-old were walking down a corridor of the University looking for Dr. Kelly, a member of the faculty. When they came to his door, which is just opposite mine, they found it locked, and I heard the mother say, "Oh, I'd hoped to find him in. I wonder when he'll be back." Then the small child-voice asked, "Is Dr. Kelly white or colored?"

I could not resist stepping out in the corridor and inviting them to wait in my office. As we sat, I engaged the little girl in conversation. "I heard you ask if Dr. Kelly was white or colored. Would you like it better if he were white or if he were colored?"

The mother intervened, smiling, "Laurie, it's not important if he's white or colored, is it?" The child just looked at her. Apparently, it was important to Laurie, or she would not have asked the question. Now what was she to say? "I don't know where she gets that," her mother said.

Later conversation brought out that Laurie had pretty strong feelings about race: she refused to attend a neighborhood school where she would be the only Black child in the class. Where did she get this? Where did she not! Talk about race was all around her! Yet she had to learn how to deal with her mother's obvious discomfort in talking about it in public, with the apparent contradiction between her mother's *feelings* and what her mother *said* she felt. Eventually she would make some accommodation in the matter. But the chances are that all her years of formal education would not provide formal education in this area of knowledge and skill.

If Laurie had the chance to take part in a simulated life experience, in which role-players responded with discomfort and avoidance to a racial situation, she might

1. Learn to recognize the adult behavior for what it is.
2. Learn to express her own feelings about the situation.
3. Learn how best to respond to the situation to achieve her own objectives.

Laurie, in effect, begins to learn early in her life that she can make decisions, that there are differential consequences of differential courses of behavior, and that people can be free to make their own choices of behaviors. Perhaps, just tangentially, she may learn how to make choices that are different from her parents' choices, and at the same time not feel compelled to reject her parents for their behavior.

Simulation is Safe

One of the most valuable results of role-playing is that the participants (and this includes those who are watching the role-playing) can experience the consequences of their own behavior in a relatively safe situation. Very often, people will blithely recommend a course of action in a situation, imagining what the consequences of adopting that action will be. When the recommended action is actually tried by role-playing, the imagined consequences often are not produced. Instead, the role-players respond in unexpected ways, and the person who originally thought he had the problem solved must re-think his course of action. Role-playing, then, becomes a sort of reality-testing, and the consequences of making a mistake are not very painful. Best of all, one need not be saddled with the consequences of a mistake in judgment. It is possible to expunge the error and "live" again and again through the situation, trying on new sets of behaviors until one achieves the result he has sought. In the process, he also learns the many ways in which people might respond in the situation, so that, whatever happens in real life, he is not caught completely off guard.

Trying on Different Roles

One of the great values offered by role-playing is the chance to try a new behavior that is "out of character." Often, a person sees himself as a certain type of personality with a specific repertory of behaviors suited to that personality. He cannot imagine expressing anger, for example, if he sees himself as always staying cool. In role-playing he can "try on" the angry behavior and get the feel of it, see if he likes it and if it seems suitable for him. He may find that expressing anger fills some great needs for him and that he has been depriving himself of fulfilling those needs because he thought the expression of anger was not part of his personality.

Similarly, a child who is forever seen by his classmates as the clown may try on the role of the serious student. Not only may he see himself in a new way—and like it—but his classmates may suddenly recognize his potential for new ways of behaving. They may, as a result, *permit* him to change his overall behavior, as they did not when they responded only to his clowning.

Of course, there are the obvious opportunities for trying different roles. Students play parents, Blacks play whites and vice versa, and generally people can live for a little while in the shoes of someone they are trying to know better. (I think we have not reached that point in our maturity as a society where we can have boys role-play girls. Perhaps until boys are generally able to do this we will not be able to solve most of the problems of discrimination against women.)

Preparation for Preparation

Teachers seem forever to be concerned about "preparing" children for every new classroom activity that is suggested to them. They seem to think that the new activity must be engaged in "successfully," and, to insure this success, other things must first be done with the children. This may be true if the new activity depends upon skills that the children must learn first, so that the activity becomes a culmination of the learning of a number of other skills in developmental sequence. Often, however, the activity itself is merely an opportunity to learn certain new behaviors, and the children become better at it as they engage in it.

Thus, role-playing need not be entered into with great trepidation, with the teacher cautiously "preparing" the children by having them engage in other activities first. If the role-playing situations are familiar enough to them, they will enter into the spirit of it, and find solutions to the problems presented.

I have seen teachers work on pantomiming as a preparation for role-playing. I have seen children learning parts and putting on a play as "good discipline" before getting into role-playing. I have heard children discuss and discuss endlessly the idea of role-playing. Some of the preparation, like putting on a play, causes students to confuse the objectives of the different activities and miss the point of role-playing. For example, they may be compelled to write scripts and rehearse for role-playing, and it will be difficult to help them see the difference between the two activities.

It might also be kept in mind that too much "preparation" for an activity may leave the children bored with the whole idea of that activity before they ever have a chance to try it!

The Dangers of Education

Occasionally, a teacher who engages in role-playing for the first time expresses reluctance to use it with children because "it can be dangerous." Let me hasten to assure them that education *is* a dangerous activity. When we try to teach children to read and they do not learn, we may be doing permanent damage to their personalities. When we expose them to mathematics and they fail, we may be marking them for a lifetime of failure. When we teach them about drugs, one or two of them may be moved to do some personal experimentation. When we free them from the fears of sex, some may—in the first flush of relief—engage in some sexual activity they have not tried before.

Yes, learning is a very dangerous activity and the teacher is accessory to it. It opens the person up to new ideas and new experiences. It causes great discomfort as old and comfortable ways are abandoned and new behaviors tried. It encourages the taking of risks in new relationships. It exchanges complacency and even serenity for excitement and anger, anguish and exultation. Or, at least, it *should* do all of these things!

Some Situations for Role-playing

Situation Number 1: Race Relations

Sometimes, teachers seek justification for doing role-playing when they should be teaching mathematics or English. There is no reason why significant problem-solving should not go on in any subject matter area of the curriculum. For example, here is a role-playing situation written and used by a shop teacher.

Mr. Smith, a Black man, comes into the office of Mr. Jones. Mr. Jones is the personnel director of a large company. The company is growing and has many jobs available. Mr. Smith is well qualified for one of the jobs but Mr. Jones tells him that he cannot have it. Mr. Smith asks "why."

Traditionally, the shop class involved using lathes and other machinery for building things. The pupils had never discussed the time when they would be trying to find jobs with the skills they were learning. The shop curriculum did not provide for such learning. However, the teacher became convinced that he had a responsibility to extend the curriculum somewhat.

The objective of the lesson was to enable the youngsters—boys of fifteen and sixteen—to experience vicariously a job situation in which they are discriminated against, and to enable them to practice responding to the apparent discrimination in a constructive way.

Situation Number 2: Race Relations

Joe and Peter go to an all white school in the suburbs of a large city. One day two Black students, Jack and Steve, transfer from one of the city schools to Joe's and Peter's classes. Joe and Peter try to act friendly toward Jack and Steve, but their overtures seem to be ignored by the two Black boys.

Several days later, Joe and Peter are running down the steps after school, hurrying to catch their bus. Jack and Steve just happen to be passing that way, and by what seems to be an accident, Jack bumps into Peter and Peter's books fall to the floor to be scattered by other hurrying students. Peter screams at Jack, "You dirty nigger, can't you watch where you're going?"

Objectives

To get some idea of the feelings of being Black and surrounded by whites in a new situation.

To understand one's own hostility at being rebuffed.

To learn to deal with people who use racial epithets.

To understand one's own feelings of hostility against another race.

Situation Number 3: Drug Use

It is 12:30 A.M., a Friday evening in Summer. Two groups of young people in two separate cars are leaving different parties in a predominantly white neighborhood. One group is white, the other made up of both Black and white people. Everyone has had a good time, they are feeling good and are a little loud and boisterous. Some singing and loud talk occurs as they drive along with open windows. A rumor that drug pushers have been active in the area has the police more alert than usual. Eventually both cars are stopped by the police at different points and the occupants questioned.

Objectives

To reveal differential expectation of drug use among white and racially mixed groups.

To reveal attitudes toward police.

To learn how to deal with negative expectations on the part of police.

Situation Number 4: Sex Education

Miss Green has asked eight of her pupils to stay in the room and have lunch with her, so that they may have a discussion afterwards. They are delighted to do this, and later, in the midst of a discussion about "how far should one go on the first date," Mr. Smith, the Vice-Principal comes in. He stands and listens a while and then stomps out, visibly disturbed.

That afternoon he stops Miss Green on her way out of the building and asks her if she would mind coming into his office for a few minutes. Then he says, "Miss Green, I'm surprised at you! How could you let your students talk about such things! No wonder we have problems in the school."

Objectives

To learn to deal with administrators' resistance to sex education.

To learn how to teach youngsters how to deal with adults who resist a realistic approach to problems of sex.

Situation Number 5: Intergroup Relations

In a mixed class of Mexican, Anglo, and some Indian students there is one boy who is constantly causing a class disruption. The teacher, an Anglo man, can finally cope with him no longer and writes out an office pass. As the boy waits for the pass he says, "You just hate me 'cause I'm a Mexican! You never pick on the Anglos! Why's it always me? You're prejudiced!"

Objectives

To look at one's own professional behavior objectively.

To understand the feelings of a Mexican child in an Anglo world.

To try to deal with disruptive behavior in terms of causes rather than just symptomatically.

To learn useful ways of dealing with hostility.

To learn useful ways of dealing with prejudice.

Testimonials from Students of All Ages

Japanese-American high school student who has just role-played a situation in which he delivered a stinging condemnation against white attitudes toward Orientals in southeast Asia: "I never thought I could say such things out loud. I feel so light—like a load off my head."

Second-grade Black student who played the role of a white boy: "I felt great! No wonder whites act mean! It makes you feel big!"

Middle-aged Black school counselor who observed a scene where a Black couple were refused service in a restaurant: "Let me play it! This happened to me and all I did was suffer in silence! Let me show you what I would do now!"

Senior in high school who played the role of a father: "I thought I would understand my son, but he made me so mad I just wanted to punish him."

Sixth-grade girl who played a sixth-grade girl talking to her hygiene teacher: "It was so easy! Why didn't I ever tell her how dumb that hygiene class is!"

6

Words and Phrases That Hurt

Description of the Technique

Borrow several geoboards from the mathematics teacher. (Geo-boards are flat squares of wood into which small nails have been hammered half-way at intervals of one inch, so that they look something like a miniature fakir's bed of nails. They are generally used to teach children something about plane geometry by stretching rubber bands into different shapes between nails.) Stretch a rubber band from the nail in the center of the top row to the nail in the center of the bottom row. This is the starting position.

Now, divide the class into groups of eight to ten people, preferably with each group around a small table. If tables are not available, have them sit in a circle with an empty chair in the middle. Place a geoboard and a set of cards face down in the center of each table. (On each card is written an item from the list *Words and Phrases that Hurt*.)

Then:

1. One at a time, each player turns up a card and reads it aloud.

2. Immediately, someone in the group extends the rubber band two spaces in any direction. (Increasing the tension in the rubber band is merely a symbolic portrayal of the tension that is built up when a member of a minority group hears the remark.)

3. The players discuss the remark, trying to understand the cause of the tension build-up. Since these items have been culled from the first-hand experiences of minority-group members, the players cannot as a group conclude that there is nothing tension-producing about the remark. If no one can understand why it annoys people, then the teacher who is circulating from group to group may be called on to give additional information.

4. When the players have some idea of the significance of the remark, they then try to determine what could be said or done to ameliorate a situation in which such a remark is made. Here players have often found it useful, without necessarily leaving their seats, to role-play specific instances where such things are said, so that they may more clearly see the result of any ameliorating action. (If this game is first played after the pupils have been involved in role-playing, they do this spontaneously. If they don't, it is good to get them started role-playing early in the game.) The objectives of such action are a) to help the target of the insult come away with his self-concept undamaged, b) to help the insulter and any bystanders learn the significance of what has been said, and c) to discourage people from saying such things.

5. If the players can think of an ameliorating response, they may go on to the next card. (It is better to limit the time spent on each card to about five minutes, or the "game" feeling is lost and the group just engages in discussion that may get further and further away from the objectives.) If all they can decide is that the remark should never have been said, they must extend the rubber band one more space, (because hindsight is of limited value). They may never move the rubber band back because no matter how much everybody has learned in the situation, damage has been done by the original expression of prejudice.

6. Each time a rubber band breaks (or the players are afraid

to stretch the rubber band any more) add one to the group score.

7. When all the cards have been played, the group with the lowest score wins.

WORDS AND PHRASES THAT HURT
(for Race and Ethnic Relations)

1. We must have *law* and *order*.
2. To a Black person: Why, you have several mayors representing you now! One in Cleveland, one in Newark . . .
3. A white woman asking just about any Black woman she knows: Do you know someone who would help me do my housework?
4. A white person to a Black person: You can make your school as good as ours.
5. A white teacher about Puerto Rican children: Why should I teach them? They'll never get anywhere.
6. A teacher about poor children: If we let them take the books home, they'll just get them dirty and destroy them.
7. A white person: Some of my best friends are Negroes.
8. A white person to a Black acquaintance: You're different from most Negroes I know.
9. About any group: They *all* do that.
10. A white person to a Black person: Why do you want to send your children to our schools?
11. Upon announcing one's intention to "integrate" a job situation: Of course, we will make sure we hire a *qualified* Negro.
12. A white person to a Black person: Your people are so happy all the time.
13. A white person to a Black person: I don't understand what you people want.
14. To a minority-group person as he applies for a job at 7:30 A.M.: You should have gotten here five minutes sooner. We just hired someone for that job.
15. To an Italian person by someone who is not Italian: Why, you don't *look* Italian.

16. Referring to a Black man: You know the boy I mean.
17. A white person to a Black person: I know you're proud of Thurgood Marshall.
18. A mainlander to a Puerto Rican: I think your people should get together and agree to help each other.
19. A white person: Our old neighborhood used to be good when I lived there as a kid, but look at it now!
20. A white person to a Black person: The death of Martin Luther King was a terrible loss to your race.
21. An Anglo about Mexican people: Why don't they take care of their own, like we did?
22. To a Jewish person, by someone who is not Jewish: I didn't know you were Jewish—you don't act like one.
23. Said to a Black nurse: Do you like this better than housework?
24. A white to an Indian: I think your people have made great progress.

Rationale for the Technique

General Objectives

The game has a number of purposes in the teaching of race relations. However, with a little imagination card items can be developed for dealing with other intergroup and interpersonal relationships. The essential objectives of the game remain the same:

1. To say aloud in a safe group situation words that insult, annoy, make angry, hurt.
2. To reinforce the idea that, though everyone does not have these feelings when hearing the words, the fact is that many people do.
3. To give opportunity for learning why people use these words and why others respond emotionally to them.
4. To give opportunity for developing strategies for dealing with people who say these words.
5. To develop conviction in those who are the target that there is nothing wrong with them.

We are not concerned here with the obvious ethnic and racial epithets that people purposely use to insult and denigrate. Perhaps it is not too optimistic to say that they are rapidly disappearing from use, not necessarily because prejudice is disappearing but because it is no longer fashionable to be openly prejudiced. The evidences or prejudice these days are more subtle, though to the victims they remain quite clear. The job of education is to make them equally clear to everyone else and also to undo the effects of such prejudice on the people against whom it is directed.

Encouraging the Expression of Feelings

Generally, the pattern of relations between groups in this country has been such that, when a person is hurt or angered by one of these remarks, the chances are that he bites his lip and says nothing until he gets back to people of his own group. He pays a price for this in unrelieved anger, frustration, and self-doubt. In the course of this game, the minority-group person who feels the sting of these remarks can express his anger in the presence of the other group. He can say in no uncertain terms how he feels about implications and assumptions—no matter how subtle—that he should be grateful for white concessions or white attempts to relegate him to a white-defined place in American society.

White people in the class also are encouraged to give voice to feelings about intergroup situations. They can express the kind of discomfort that compels them to say, in an awkward attempt to be friendly, "Oh, I envy you! You people are always so happy and carefree." And they can express outrage and anger that their good intentions are so unkindly rebuffed. Often, both Blacks and whites are surprised at the existence of these emotions. They have been talking for most of their lives about the need for mutual understanding and mutual acceptance and they have been unaware of those very feelings that most effectively prevented any but the most superficial rapprochement between the races.

Imagine a situation like this: It is election day in the city. School, however, is in session as usual and at lunchtime the teachers are sitting in a corner of the lunchroom for their half-hour of relaxation. One of the two Black teachers in the school is there too. The conversation turns naturally to the election and conjecture about who will be the next mayor. The Black teacher has not said much, perhaps because she is still somewhat wary about the attitude towards her. (She has not been in the school for very long.) In an effort to bring her into the conversation one of the other teachers turns to her and says brightly, "You have several mayors representing you now, don't you? One in Cleveland, another in Newark, Gary, Indiana. . . ."

Now what is there to annoy anyone in such a knowledgeable, friendly effort at giving credit and recognition where they are due? To the Black person who hears this, however, it sounds unmistakably like a protestation that the speaker is not prejudiced against him. See, I have no negative feelings about Black mayors, or about you. The need to make such an avowal casts serious doubt on its accuracy. Shakespeare said it all about protesting too much and in this case a little protestation is too much.

There is something else involved here that is calculated to put a person's back up. The assumption that Black mayors represent Black people is rarely coupled with the assumption that white mayors represent white people. As a matter of fact, the attempt in American politics has been to sell the idea that, regardless of race, an elected official represents all the people. This is the argument that has often been used to resist the demand by Black voters that Black candidates be added to party rosters. But now that some Black mayors are elected the feeling of whites is that these officials represent Black people. And not only the Black voters of their own constituencies, but Black people everywhere! Black people hear in this the implication that Blacks are unable to be fair, to be representative, to function politically in a democracy. (It is analogous to the assumption, still rife, that Black jurymen will inevitably find for a Black defendant. This assumption has resulted in Blacks being systematically excluded from jury duty in many places. The documented evidence, however, that whites persistently mete out differential justice to Blacks, has not resulted in excluding whites from jury duty.)

If only minority-group people are playing the game, the expression of anger is, of course, no new experience. However, the fact that opportunity for it is provided in a school setting has a tendency to switch the focus from merely expressing anger to considering how the general social situation may be changed. The teacher also is in a position to encourage pupils to examine data that make it clear that those who are the victims of prejudice and discrimination are not the cause of their own victimization.

For example, primary school children are often refused permission to take home their textbooks because teachers feel that poor children, Black children, don't care about books and destroy them wantonly. It is not at all unlikely that the children come away believing that there is really some thing wrong them them that they are not permitted to take books home. How do they know that 1) they haven't been given the chance to take the books, so how can anyone determine that they are book-destroyers? 2) people *learn* to take care of books by using them, owning them, borrowing them and finally appreciating their value, and 3) that they also are entitled to the opportunity to learn? Later in life, the adult may realize intellectually that the proscription against taking books home was based on prejudice and inequality of educational opportunity, but the emotional scar may still be there and the self-doubt may never be completely erased.

Early in life children need to learn to resist the process that makes them doubt themselves. Freely expressing their feelings of outrage, humiliation and anger at this kind of treatment is a sound first step in beginning to examine the realistic causes of prejudice and discrimination.

Analogies can be drawn here with relationships between adults and young people. The circular kind of griping that goes on within each group about the frailties and defects of the other group merely perpetuates the separation and the lack of understanding and acceptance. In sex education and drug education the optimum approach would be to bring young people and their elders together to begin to understand each others' doubts, fears and angers. However, usually the best we can do is work only with youngsters in school. Then we must encourage the free expression of feelings and build on this freedom acceptance of those feelings. With self-acceptance, young people can begin to plan how to get adults into cooperative efforts for dealing with problems of sex and drugs.

Thus, one of the items on the list of *Words and Phrases That Hurt* (for drug education), is, "You must admit that people who use marijuana or other drugs are just weak." If 11 percent of the children above sixth grade have used drugs at one time or another (as one study indicates), such a statement is calculated to stir anger in many of them. The game permits them to put the anger into words without fear of reprisal, and then sets them to determining on the best way to deal with the situation. Should they clam up and so cut off all further communication with the adult? Should they defend the drug users vehemently and thus risk condemnation and rejection? Should they offer some facts on drug use? Should they admit to having used drugs? Should they go out and use drugs as an act of retaliation against unjust judgment? It is possible here to examine all these alternatives seriously, sharing information and opinions, testing out differential behaviors in simulated experiences, and weighing outcomes. The eventual choice of a course of action can then be drawn from a repertory of considered choices rather than from momentary emotion and impulse. This is not because emotion has been dissipated, but because it has been expressed, accepted and built upon.

Developing Empathy

One of the objectives of education is to add to an individual's knowledge and sensitivity what other people have learned in the course of their own lives. If our life decisions are based only on what we have ourselves experienced first-hand, we are at a severe disadvantage because everything we experience is filtered through our own unique perceptions. In the process of educating ourselves, we can open ourselves to awareness of other people's perceptions. We can compare other people's perceptions with our own. Eventually we can begin to get some feeling for what other people are experiencing. In this way we broaden the basis of our perceptions and judgments.

In the course of trying to determine why these remarks are resented, students who never saw anything wrong with them get some feeling for the feelings of others. They may not realize that when they say, "I don't understand what you people want," it is really not merely a confession of ignorance. It is usually perceived by the listener as a diatribe against 1) people who are separated by a wall from the speaker ("You people" are a wall away!), 2) people who appear to be demanding more than other people have, and 3) people who are already getting everything they are entitled to.

Often students are able to experience other people's anger at such a remark in the course of the game and to feel a responsive anger in themselves. When they role-play various situations in attempts to find alternate ways of dealing with these remarks and with the anger they provoke, they can actually act out anger and frustration in roles they may never have taken in real life.

With these kinds of experiences, it becomes less likely that an individual will perceive one of the situations merely in terms of his own life. He will no longer respond with impatience to others who are hurt and angered by perceived snubs and insults. He will not glibly write off Black people, for instance, with the comment: "Oh, he walks around with a chip on his shoulder." Nor will he contribute to the "generation gap" by believing that it is no use trying to make adults understand. From the vantage-point of other people's shoes, he will be more understanding of them even if he does not agree with them. He will of course also be more aware of the significance of what he himself is saying: He will no longer deceive himself into believing that he is free of prejudice and hostility.

Testing Behaviors for Dealing with Prejudice

Expressing anger is helpful. Understanding other people's anger is equally valuable. However, it is necessary to take another step if a great number of anger-provoking situations are to be eliminated from our lives. We must ask the questions: "When somebody insults me, what do I *do* about it?" "When I hear someone insult someone else, what do I *do* about it?" "When I discover that I have, unknowingly, been using insulting remarks, what do I *do* about it?" Then it is necessary to *do* something, to take some action in real-life situations.

There is evidence that, when people insult someone in terms of his group membership ("You Jews"), they are moved to reconsider their behavior when a third person objects to the insult. However, one may doubt his own ability to say something appropriate on the spur of the moment or one may feel anxiety about what the response to intervention might be. Here, in the relative safety of the classroom, the pupil may get a feeling for various modes of intervention, and also have a chance to see how different people might respond to what he says or does. Then when he is faced with the necessity for doing something in a more public situation he is not caught completely unprepared.

For example, he may hear a white person say, "Our old neighborhood used to be good when I lived there as a kid, but just look at it now!" The implication and the insult here is that Black people who now live in the neighborhood have caused its deterioration. What could another white person, hearing this and recognizing the insult, say or do to ameliorate the situation? Suppose he decides to point out that neighborhoods inevitably age, and with age comes a natural deterioration; Black people finally have access to a neighborhood fifty or sixty years after it was new, after several generations of white people have reared their children and departed. Suppose he adds that houses in most such neighborhoods are usually bought up by speculators and landlords who cut up single-dwelling homes into multiple units, which means that there are four, five, and six times as many Black people as there used to be white people in the same space. This naturally increases the rate of deterioration. And he can give still more information: about how these multiple-unit dwellings are rented to people (renters, with no property investment, do not put money into maintenance); and how the landlords do not provide adequate maintenance or repairs (city agencies are woefully deficient in enforcing landlord responsibility).

How will the person whose insult started it all react to this information? Will he get angry? Will he listen to the end and reconsider his insult? Will he try to justify his point of view? Will he walk away after the first few words? Obviously, different people will respond differently. One way of experiencing these different responses is to try them out on each other. One person in the group may react with anger, another may listen and think. And the person who chose information-giving as a way of dealing with insult (that he obviously assumed was the result of ignorance) has an opportunity to deal with the different responses in a variety of ways.

Similarly, when a Puerto Rican is told by a mainlander, "I think your people should get together and agree to help each other," he may feel fury well up in him at the presumptuousness of an outsider telling him what Puerto Ricans should do. He may feel humiliated and embarrassed because other people are hearing this and he feels unable to say anything. He may be afraid to answer because the mainlander may be in a position of power, or it may be a social situation that he does not want to disrupt, or he is just afraid of expressing anger against someone who is not Puerto Rican. He may, of course, feel only contempt and decide that the mainlander merits no answer at all. In the course of this game he can test out a number of responses and finally choose the ones that seem to have the results he wants. In the process he may discover that he is not really powerless to speak or take action. He may learn that results that may have seemed dangerous in his mind are really not so dangerous when they are brought out into the open.

Sense of Control and Success in School

Children who are consistently snubbed, insulted and excluded because of their race, religion or nationality can develop a sense of impotence, a feeling that fate has condemned them to suffer in this way and that there is nothing they can do about it. Their response to this feeling of powerlessness may be a blind anger directed against the world or a fearful withdrawal from the world. Either way, they become convinced that the good things in the world are possible only through luck and that personal efforts to achieve are useless.

The connection between this conviction and success in school is obvious. If one is powerless to affect one's fate, then why bother trying to succeed? Effort to change the throw of the dice is effort wasted. Many teachers of minority children have responded with incredulous frustration to the complete indifference of the children to threats of failing grades and expulsion from school. When they were children, the teachers believed that achievement in school led to success in life, and their belief has been substantiated. They cannot understand why the children in their classes are only indifferent when they hold out the carrot of success to them. They do not know that, while the children want success as much as the teachers did, they actually do not believe that their own personal efforts will bring them such success.

More Words and Phrases That Hurt

Young people often feel snubbed and insulted by adults and by a society that sometimes seems bent on ridiculing and punishing them and excluding them from meaningful participation. They may respond with destructive anger or withdrawal. Their feeling of powerlessness to change their condition leads many of them to give up altogether on setting goals for themselves. They feel the government has been unresponsive to their protests against war, and so many have stopped protesting. They see big business dragging its feet in preventing pollution and waste of resources, so they have abandoned many of their ecological activities. From problems of poverty and racism, they often see no way out. (One young woman exclaimed to me with obvious pain the other day, "I'm twenty-six years old and I've never voted for anyone who was elected! I'm against violence, but I can't see any other way of getting people into government who care about what's happening!")

If from early childhood people can learn to deal directly and effectively with the snubs and insults, they may establish and maintain communication with adults so that the "generation gap" may not continue to be a chasm of blank misunderstanding and silence. Undoubtedly there will always be a gap of perception and opinion between generations but there is no reason why they cannot continue to talk about their differences and learn from each other—one to profit from the errors of the past, the other to utilize the expanding knowledge of the present. Establishing and maintaining communication also helps reduce the build-up of resentment and anger that is generated when people are forced to keep silent in the face of insult. And as people learn to manage successfully the external challenges with which they are faced, they develop feelings of control over the environment and over their own destinies.

Here are more samples of words and phrases that hurt young people. They revolve around drug use, attitudes toward sex, and attitudes toward young people generally. Obviously they are generally said by adults. Pupils, given the opportunity, can probably add substantially to the lists out of their own experience.

WORDS AND PHRASES THAT HURT
(for Drug Education)

1. You must admit that people who use marijuana and other drugs are just weak.
2. Children who use drugs break their parents' hearts.

3. You should have nothing at all to do with people who use drugs, not even those who have used them once.
4. Once a person has used drugs, you can't trust him when he says he has stopped using them.
5. All those hippies and demonstrators are drug addicts.

WORDS AND PHRASES THAT HURT
(for Sex Education)

1. What do you kids know about what's right, anyhow?
2. When you're older, you'll understand.
3. Wearing short skirts or hot pants is just an invitation to sexual promiscuity.
4. My generation cared about morality and decency, not like this generation!
5. You want rights and freedom but you're not willing to assume any responsibility.

Some Student Responses to the Game

The Satisfaction of Expressing Anger

Over and over again, in using this technique with people of different ages and groups, what has impressed me is the great feeling of relief that becomes apparent when victims of insult and exclusion have been able to verbalize their anger in a relatively safe situation. This is not to say that they have not expressed anger before but generally they have not done so in a school setting, in the environment of the "establishment." Opportunity to do so lends a certain validity to the anger and implies a recognition and acceptance of it by society and so seems to reduce some of the frustrations that the justifiably angry people feel.

Also the outpouring of anger leaves inner space for reason and creativity to begin to move so that people are able to set themselves to the task of solving the problems. They come away from the game smiling with satisfaction, apparently feeling that they have made some contribution to alleviating bad situations. They are often amazed that they were able to think of things to do and say in situations that they had given up as hopeless.

New Light on the Hurters

When two ethnic groups are represented in the class, those habitually victimized by the words and phrases are surprised when the habitual insulters begin to offer suggestions for dealing with the insults. "When I say 'you people,' " one white student said, "let me know. I probably often say it without realizing it. I'd appreciate your doing that until I get rid of the habit."

One parent admitted, "When I say, 'You'll understand when you're older,' it's only because I can't seem to explain that I feel the fear and pity and sadness. I'm afraid I'll be laughed at. If I could know that young people wouldn't ridicule my feelings, I'd feel freer to talk—and to listen."

Often, the victims come away feeling less victimized, more aware that the hurters are hurting too.

The "Ah-hah!" Response of Whites

Once, while playing the game, some white players were insisting that the trouble between Black people and white people was primarily that Black people were too tight, too ready to feel insult where none was intended. As the discussion and role-playing proceeded, a white student playing the part of a Black person burst into anger at hearing for the third time, "You have to earn your rights, and with rights come responsibilities." She shouted, "Earn our rights?! Did you fight for Independence? We did, too. Did you work until you dropped? We did for centuries without pay! Did your sons die in all the other wars? Ours did! What have you done to earn your rights that we haven't?!"

Suddenly her face showed a look of perfect understanding. She *knew* what was making Black people angry—really knew it for the first time.

7

A System for Community Involvement

Introduction

As we have noted, for the poor child, and particularly the poor Black and Puerto Rican child, the motivation to succeed in school is closely tied to his sense of control over his own life. (See Coleman et al., *Equality of Educational Opportunity*.) In education in the past there has been almost no attempt to intervene directly in the development of this sense of control or in the development of the child's self-concept. Community involvement can help the teacher develop methods and materials for such intervention.

For example, if the child who feels trapped in the quagmire of poverty and racism can discover what people in his own community are doing to change things, he can begin to see some place for himself in that process of change. But unless the teacher knows what the people in the community are doing and has caught some of the feelings of excitement, hope, despair and frustration, he cannot communicate any of this to the children. Nor can he help the child find his place in the pattern of action.

Knowledge of the community cannot be gleaned from traditional textbooks. The community itself must be the primary source that the teacher studies. Such knowledge is vitally needed to make contact with the child in some elementary and basic ways. A simple instance deals with the universal teacher practice of using examples from life to illustrate ideas, make comparisons and reinforce learnings. Naturally the teacher will use illustrations from her own life because these are the things that have meaning for her. Involvement in the child's community will give the teacher experiences that also have meaning for the child. (A specific activity for the teacher might be: Every time you plan a lesson, include in your plan at least one reference to something you have experienced in the community.)

Often, the child lives in the community but is so caught up in his day-to-day life that he is largely unaware of some of the significant organizational activity that adults are engaged in. Just as we teach him from textbooks about things he has never heard of, so we must teach him from community life. One way to do this it to put him in touch with adults who are struggling and often getting things done. (A specific activity for the teacher: If there are community organizations working to change discriminating practices, lessons must be taught during which the teacher has opportunity to diagnose the children's educational needs in the area of race relations. Additional lessons must be taught that address themselves to those needs by introducing the child to the work of the community.)

Just as the teacher must deal with disruptive children, so the mother deals day after day with her disruptive child. Is a particular child disruptive only in class, or does his mother also have problems with him? Has his mother been able to solve some of the problems? Are her solutions usuable for the teacher? Even if the teacher finds that she cannot incorporate the information she gets into her own solution, she needs to know what the child has already experienced if she is to be successful with him. In the name of courtesy and deference to a primary source, she ought to go to see the mother instead of requesting that the mother come to see her. (A specific activity for the teacher: In writing an analysis of the educational needs of a child you are teaching, consider what you have learned about him that is not to be found in school records or noted in casual observation.)

These five suggested activities do not preclude additional activities that develop naturally from the teacher's growing knowledge of the community and his ability to use this knowledge in the education of the children.

Rationale for Involvement for the Pupil

Sense of Control

One of the differences between poor children—especially poor Black children—and white middle-class children seems to be their feelings concerning control over their own lives. While the middle-class children generally feel that they can make what they want to of their lives, the poor children more often feel that fate has put them into a bad situation, and only luck will get them out of it. They feel powerless in the face of the sources that seem to be directing their lives and they see no way in which their own efforts can change their situation. The effect on their efforts in school is obvious: if luck is the key to success, what is the good of learning reading and arithmetic? There's just no point to it.

These are the children who so desperately need the knowledge and skills developed by community involvement. They have to become aware of the fact that there are people in the community who are struggling to change their lives. The people in the struggle are friends and neighbors of theirs, even members of their own families, and they are actively engaged in organizing the community in a great variety of activities, all the way from systematic protests against government agencies to classes for learning basic academic skills.

Knowledge of such activity helps the children see that people they know, poor like themselves, have not given up on trying to change their lives. Not only that, but with their successes the people are demonstrating that change is possible. (This does not, of course, mean that the failures are to be ignored or kept from the children. On the contrary, the failures are to be examined and analyzed, so that they may be understood and the causes of them prevented in the future.)

We in education know that children need models with which to identify in order to mature and succeed in life. However, we often provide models who are so far removed from any goal they see as possible for themselves, that they can react only with cynicism and alienation. For example, the white professional or businessman is hardly the ideal model for the poor Black child. Nor is the Black professional or businessman a much better one, at least at the outset, for the many children who feel that they are so far from such goals that there is no use even trying to reach them. Such children need to become a part of the strivings and goals of people they can recognize more easily as being like them, people who are poor and who are in the process of changing their own world. Thus it is not only the single Black person who has "made it" who is to be emulated, because too often he may merely reinforce the child's reliance on luck: "This man got the breaks, but he's an exception." It is the *concerted* commitment to changing life, the process of organizing, developing powerful influences and bringing these to bear on the decision-makers, that can help the child to see that there is a place for him and a real chance of success in changing his life.

Of course, poverty and exclusion cause other problems in development and learning. The child who eats lead-base paint off the crumbling walls of a slum apartment may suffer irreversible brain damage. The child who comes to school speaking a language other than English may be viewed as uneducable. To the extent that such problems may ultimately be eliminated by active citizen involvement in the processes of social change, then to that extent it is necessary for the child to be educated in the community.

Reading the Living Textbook That Is the Community

I think there is little doubt that the textbook is the most widely-used teaching aid in the schools. There is no doubt, either, that the information that the poor child needs about his community is much too current to be found in a printed textbook. Things are happening in poor communities today that have never happened before. People who have no position in the political or professional system are emerging as articulate and skillful leaders, and they are being listened to by the mayors, the health commissioners, the superintendents of education. Protest efforts that the writers of books never envisioned are being tested in communities. Even if we read all the books as they come off the presses, there will still be more to learn *as it happens* in the community.

It is worth noting that the child who has not yet been taught to read, whether he is seven or seventeen years old, is not handicapped when he is given an assignment to learn the community. It suddenly becomes apparent that he is not "retarded" or a "slow learner." The "book" is a book that he can already read; the feeling of success that this can generate is fertile ground for continued achievement in school.

The middle-class child, too, has everything to gain from using his community as his textbook. He, too, needs a living textbook to make his years in school come alive. He, too, needs to learn what his people are doing to solve problems. Perhaps, too, his feeling of power needs to be tempered by the reality of the frustrations attendant upon communicating with the bureaucracy of government or the hierarchy of business. Middle-class people also have feelings of powerlessness, and they too need skills for planning and instituting social change.

For all children, the time must come when the first textbook (his own community) must be expanded. Contiguous communities and more and more distant ones become Books Two, Three, and Four as processes of discovery, exploration and inquiry widen his horizons. Thus, the Black child, the white child, the middle-class child and the poor child all begin to see their own communities and their own lives within a total social context.

Seeing the Meaning in School

When we try to teach a child how to solve a problem of geometry in the textbook, it may be difficult to make him see why learning to solve the problem is worthwhile. I am not at all sure that we teachers are always convinced that it is! Actually, most of us teach geometry because we learned it, and it is part of the required curriculum.

When we add to the geometry English grammar, Russian history, French grammar and algebra, then the "Why?" of school becomes too overwhelming to consider. Not very long ago, I talked to a young social studies teacher who was disturbed that her class of Black tenth-graders were not interested in learning about the Russian revolution. She saw a viable analogy between the Russian revolution and the contemporary Black revolution and she could not understand why young Black men were not eager to explore the Russian experience. Suddenly something about what she was saying gave me a flash of insight. "Have you taught them about the Black revolution?" I asked. *She had not!*

The Black Revolution was not a part of the required curriculum!

No teacher who uses the community for a textbook can make such a mistake. The Revolution in this "book" is real; it has meaning because it affects each child's life in ways he can *feel*. It frightens or confuses or pleases him or makes him angry. While he is feeling, he cannot doubt that the subject has meaning for him.

Living, not Preparing for Life

It has always seemed to me that the ultimate insult to children is to subject them to school in order to "prepare them for life." With this one cliché we deny the importance of their existence and tell them that what they are going through now is not living. If living is feeling, thinking, wanting, doing what you need to do, then we imply that what children feel, what they think, and what they want are not really worth considering until their time of preparation for living is over.

The teacher who gives children opportunity to become involved in the community gives the lie to this archaic insult. She is saying in effect, "What is happening to you matters; what is important to you *is* important; your feelings deserve consideration and response."

I would agree that the earlier years of a person's life should provide experiences for dealing with more complex problems in later life. Ordinarily, however, education in the schools really does not provide such developmental learning. Decision-making, for example, is hardly more complicated for high school students than it is for elementary school students. Curricula are predetermined, schedules are lock-step organized and student governments are neither governments nor are they run by students.

The sham of respecting students was nowhere so clearly revealed as it was in 1971 in a large city. At the instigation of high school students, a Bill of Rights for high school students was adopted by the school board. Article 9 read, "Students shall not be subjected to corporal punishment." Shortly after that, a tragic shooting of a teacher by a student impelled the board to institute corporal punishment as a policy, but for elementary students only. The board then began to ponder what punishments could be administered to high school students who were obviously too big to beat.

One serious suggestion by a member was to set up a public whipping post!

In all candor just what preparation do we give our youngsters? The technical skills for earning a living they learn on the job or outside the professional schools. Basic skills are learned only by those who are primed by experiences outside of school. Except for a few bits of information that are shortly outdated and even more quickly forgotten we teach them primarily to detest our demands for obedience and conformity and to survive overwhelming boredom.

Rationale for Involvement for the Teacher

Knowing the Students

The essential aim of community involvement for the teacher is to provide him with material for motivating children to learn in school. Axiomatic in the education of teachers is the idea that in order to motivate the child, the teacher must know him. The teacher who knows the child only in the classroom and school setting is missing some of the most important things about him. The significant adults in his life, the atmosphere in his home, the streets he walks through, and the stores he shops in all make the child what he is.

The middle-class white child taught by the middle-class white teacher is at some advantage. The teacher, even if he does not spend time in the community of the school, is in a general way probably familiar with the life style and expectations of the child. This is not to say that she certainly knows as much about the child as she needs to know. Not at all! This particular child may have a single-parent home. This other child may have an alcoholic father. This child may have an older brother who is favored in the home. This child may be getting nothing but discouragement from his parents. This child may be a genius in mechanics, a strength that simply does not become apparent in the reading-writing-recess schedule of the traditional classroom.

However, the middle-class teacher of the middle-class child generally does not make the gross errors about him that she might about poor children. Part of the reason for this is that stereotypic perceptions of poor people are pervasive in our society, and many teachers have not had opportunity to check these errors against the reality. Thus there may be the erroneous belief that poor people are apathetic, that they don't care about their children's education, a belief reinforced by the fact that they have not, in the past, flocked to parent-teacher meetings. There may be the belief that most poor people are criminals, an error perpetuated by the misleading way that statistics are reported in the media. These and other misperceptions can seriously affect the middle-class teacher's relationship with poor students. Based on her expectations, she may abandon all efforts to establish communication with a child's parents and so miss the opportunity to know what they have done to motivate the child to learn. Or, again based on how she sees the poor, she may so clearly expect their children to steal and cheat that she teaches them to see themselves in these roles.

Not only must the teacher be constantly alert to her own tendency to make errors in perception, but she must spend part of her professional life in involvement that will uproot these errors from her being. Only by really knowing parents will she learn that most parents do care about what happens to their children and that children respond to this caring with love and loyalty. Only by working side by side with the people in the community can she learn that where apathy is found on one side of the scale, on the other side is a never-ending struggle to survive and grim determination to make a better life. Children need some help in weighting the scale on the side of activity and determination. Only by spending time in the community will the teacher learn that even in the neighborhoods with the highest incidence of reported crimes the overwhelming majority of the people are not the criminals. They are the victims, among whom are numbered the children in her class.

Reading the Living Textbook That is the Community

Reliance on the textbook as the basic material in the education of the child leads us into a number of classic errors. There is a smoothness and lucidity about events that are recorded retrospectively that gives us a distorted view of life. The turmoil of things as they happen, the confusion about which came first, the zig-zag, jagged, illogical course of events simply is not conveyed by the textbooks we use. And so our teaching takes on a detachment from life that ill prepares children for dealing with life problems.

Because the textbook is made to read from front to back, we fall into the trap of teaching events chronologically. But events far removed in time from us are inevitably not as significant or important to us as are the events occurring now. Especially when we are immediately and intimately involved in these current happenings, we could not be more interested or more "motivated" to respond to them. Therefore we should start from where we are in the scheme of things, becoming involved in the community, living it, reading it as it happens to us. As the questions arise: Why is this happening? What started it? How could it have turned out differently? we can go back to past events—*but only because we want to understand the present.* The habit, then, of relying on a chronological account of "facts" is less helpful and less interesting than working back from events in which we are personally caught up. We become learners and teachers of the living process of happenings rather than of dead chronology.

There is a vitality in the textbook that is the community that no paper book can ever have. The smell of life is something words on paper can only suggest and without it in your nostrils you cannot know what it is to walk an old street, sit in the kitchen of a poor family, or be part of a meeting of angry people. The real first-hand impact of feeling is filtered out by the smooth words on paper. An adult's fear of a group of teen-agers, a Black man's anger at a white man's presumptuousness, a child's curiosity about a stranger are all feelings that a teacher can really experience only by going into the community and becoming a part of what is happening there.

Working through Misconceptions and Fears

One of the advantages the middle-class white child has whose teacher is also a middle-class white is that the teacher is not afraid to go into his community. To the white teacher, and not infrequently to the middle-class Black teacher, the home ground of the poor Black child is a menacing jungle, fraught with the danger of imminent violence to anyone who ventures out into it. Cars are parked as close to the school as possible (often in the school yard itself), lunch is eaten in the school building, and no school meetings are ever held after dark.

The children are well aware of the teachers' fears. Nor is this awareness calculated to foster open and free communication between teacher and pupil. On the contrary, most middle-class teachers are unaware of how poor Black and Puerto Rican children feel about whites, about middle-class Blacks, about their teachers. Most are still steadfast in their belief that small children are not concerned with race, that Black children are not concerned with the race of their teachers. They are unaware of the cynicism of school children who see their teachers disappear from the neighborhood as soon as the last bell rings.

There really is no way to deal with being afraid of poor people and of people of other races without getting to know and interact with them in real situations. This is the only way to know in your bones that most people are not violent, that poor people want the same things out of life that middle-class people do, that poor parents care about their children as much as middle-class parents do. When one white person walking in a poor Black neighborhood feels bombarded by hostile glares, another meets friendly eyes and warm smiles. The two might compare their experiences and try to determine what there is about *themselves* that makes the response to them so different. One teacher who first went into the neighborhood of his school determined not to show his reluctance suddenly realized that the rictus on his face might have been causing the startled looks he was getting. Another teacher was shocked into awareness when an old man sitting in front of a house asked her why she looked so angry. The tension she felt, that was imprinted on her face, made the man think she was angry with the people she was seeing, an impression not calculated to inspire friendly looks.

The misconceptions concerning poor urban neighborhoods are fostered by the media and even by "authoritative" studies. If one reads a statistical analysis of a "race" of people, one erroneously assumes that all the members of that race are patterned on the analysis. If one reads the newspaper, one expects that the people he meets will be like the people the newspaper writes about. Neither expectation is accurate. You simply do not know what the parents of your children are like until you get to know them. Though the newspapers make much of the crimes in city neighborhoods, your particular children may live in a street where everyone knows everyone else and families live like other ordinary American families. The important point is that your children *live* there and whatever misconceptions their teacher has about the neighborhood he has also about the children. (And haven't we learned in our schools of education that in order to teach effectively we must know the *whole* child?)

Here are some statements by teachers who have been teaching minority group children and who have never gone into their neighborhoods beyond the few feet from the school to the parking lot:

> Puerto Rican girls are raised to be everything to a man. If a boy say he likes her, that's all she needs—she has no hesitancy in becoming pregnant. That's why they drop out of school.

> Eighty-five percent of the children in our school are there because the parents force them to. We'll have to get the parents to force them to stay in school. After all, nobody likes school—we didn't like school when we were young. Children don't know what they want.

> These children just don't have any worthwhile learning experiences outside of school. We have to start from scratch.

Description of the System

If we accept the conception of broadening the perspective of the teacher to include the school community as a part of his education, then we must abandon the idea that such perspective may be achieved merely by relying on the traditional examination of sociological, psychological and political science constructs. We must add to the studies of theory a plan for developmental community involvement, designed to provide for the teacher 1) information about the community from residents and leaders 2) guidance in making contact with individuals and agencies in the community and working with them and 3) encouragement in efforts to find a learning-service role in the community. Throughout the plan teachers must be committed to exploring the relationship between the teacher's effectiveness in the classroom and her involvement in community affairs, and to use what they learn in the community to improve their teaching.

The teacher's involvement in the community includes also his efforts to bring the community into the school. In her visits to parents, her operation of homework centers, her teaching of adult education groups, she seeks to cooperate with parents and other adults in exploring solutions to the problems of the schools. Eventually in-depth, on-going relationships are established between teachers and community residents which will permit teachers to know what an area is like and how it feels to be a part of it. This is particularly important when the neighborhood is a low-income one.

Where the problems include unemployment and underemployment, not enough decent housing, inferior education and the difficulties encountered in influencing change, the teacher can work side by side with the people in the community in their efforts to develop saleable skills, make contact with government agencies responsible for housing and maintenance violations, and become involved in the functions of the schools and other community agencies. She can teach basic skills to adults who want this. She can inform adults about what their children are doing in school. She can draw parents into attending school meetings and doing volunteer work in schools. Teachers can become a part of community organizations working to improve the living situation and participate in discussions on race relations and how to effect changes. They can then use their new skills and knowledge to work with children in classrooms, in extra-curricular and out-of-school situations to teach them the same skills and help them develop the self-confidence necessary to enable them to take a hand in their own destinies.

The Plan

This is the system for community involvement that teachers and prospective teachers may use to get to know their children's community. It is designed specifically for teachers who work where the people are poor. However, it can be used with minor variations for becoming a part of any school's community.

The experiences are set up developmentally to provide a teacher first with opportunities to become aware of community, then to deal with his own reactions to it, and finally to get involved in the lives of the people. It is advisable for several teachers to work on this plan together so that they may share ideas and feelings with each other and begin to define their roles in the community.

Stage 1

Objective: to react subjectively to specific situations.

Purposes

1. To effect catharsis. Experiences will trigger expressions of feelings, not only about immediate situations, but about poor people, other races, and white people.
2. To enable you to relate the differences in feelings to different levels of individual experience with poor people.
3. To begin to distinguish in poverty situations those areas of comfort and positive value, for people who do not live in the community.

Experiences

1. Walk around the school boundary and map it. (It should be a perceptions map to aid memory in recalling feelings and impressions, not a lesson in geography.)

   Identify four square blocks in the vicinity of your school and draw a line map of them on a sheet of paper. One day don't leave for home at dismissal time, but plan to spend half an hour after school walking slowly through those four square blocks. Every so often, pop into a grocery store, a coffee shop, or any other place where you can jot down a few notes. On the line map you have drawn, note briefly your perceptions as your passed various landmarks. For example: "Store-front church: I wonder what denomination it is. Teenagers on corner: They frighten me. A woman sitting on step of house smiles: Makes me feel a little more comfortable. A row of attractively kept houses: Never thought they'd be here in the midst of poverty."

   Whatever you do, don't walk around the neighborhood with a notebook, observing and writing as you go. How would you feel if strangers walked about your home neighborhood obviously observing you and making notes on your behavior? Nor should people walk in large groups, calling attention to themselves and what they are doing. There is an element of rudeness in this kind of "invasion" that people legitimately resent.

As you walk, note places you think you might like to visit and find out more about on another day.

At home again, at your leisure or perhaps in the company of the other teachers who have done this, examine your perceptions. Ask yourself what scares you and why. Ask yourself how your fears affect your teaching of the children who live in this neighborhood. Has your walk raised questions that you would like answered? How will you go about getting the answers? Do the questions deal with sociology? Economics? History? Mathematics? All of these? It is a pretty good textbook, isn't it, that demonstrates the interrelatedness of all disciplines and encourages you to go on with your studies?

2. Visit some of the places you passed on your perception-map walk. For example:

Bars (girls use Ladies' entrance!) (For people who speak easily to strangers)

Community center (For those who are more comfortable visiting in a group)

Laundromat (For people who prefer to listen)

Beauty salon

Super market

Neighborhood stores

Housing project office

Government Agencies (Federal, State, local)

Barber shop

YMCA

Real estate agent

Churches

Library

Thrift stores

You will note that the system provides for different learning styles of individuals. Some people like to go alone, some in groups; some need to be introduced; some listen, some talk. Start by doing what is most comfortable for you.

3. Visit a police station and speak to policemen on duty. Sit and watch the activities for a while. (Maybe your police chief will arrange for you to ride in a police car around the area.)

4. Visit at least two places identified in your walk, introducing yourself as a teacher temporarily assigned to (Blank) School who wants to get to know the people whose children he will be teaching. You may want to spend several hours visiting or just a few minutes. You ought to make advance appointments for these visits.

5. Visit the junior high schools fed by the elementary school and the high school fed by those junior high schools. Talk to a few teachers and students. You may want to chat about these general subjects:

    How well prepared are the children who enter your school?

    What courses do the children generally select?

    What is the nature of the counseling the children get for selecting courses?

    How do you individually and your school as an institution relate to our elementary school?

    How do you see the role of the parents in the school?

A suggestion: It is more desirable to chat informally rather than to ask a series of questions as if you were conducting an interview. *Don't take notes.*

Stage 2

Objective: To experience in some detail an effort of poor people to change their situation.

Purposes

1. To begin to develop empathy with individuals in different social classes and ethnic groups.

2. To begin to see historical and psycho-social cause and effect relationships in situations and behaviors of other groups.

Experiences

1. Pick a single organization or agency that demonstrates one of the following structural types:
   a. Outside impetus for change.
   b. Self-directed impetus for change.
   c. Self-directed impetus for change on a more sophisticated level.
   d. Self-directed impetus for change utilizing various levels of community participation.
   e. An organization that provides opportunity for community-authority relationships.
2. Make a study of how the organization got started:
   a. The first people who saw the need.
   b. What they did initially to get support for the idea.
   c. Who became involved in the secondary steps.
   d. How the organization began to take form.
   e. The relationship of the original perceived need and the current structure and function of the organization.
3. Regularly meet with your colleagues to compare notes.
4. Finally, as a group, arrive at some generalizations about how a community organizes.

Stage 3

Objective: To develop understanding of the correlation between home, community and school, defining the roles of child, parents, teacher, administrator, and the interrelationship of each with others, and of each with the inner and the total community.

Purposes

1. To develop knowledge of the total life situation of the child.

2. To relate this knowledge to his learning process.
3. To observe differential responses of children in and out of school.
4. To develop some knowledge of language differences.

Experiences

Arrange for a series of experiences that will provide opportunity to know a child in a variety of settings outside the school.

1. Regular home visits to a number of children, to chat with parents about the needs of the child.
2. Visits with the public health and social workers to one or two families with multiple problems.
3. Tutoring a child or two in his home.
4. Taking small groups of children (with some parents) to make their own contacts outside their home community. (To the city's human relations agency, to main police headquarters, to the mayor's complaint office, to the office of the legislative representative, and so on.)
5. Spending some time in a neighborhood playground speaking to the children, organizing games and generally developing relationships with them on an informal basis.
6. Taking a number of youngsters to local eye clinics and other health clinics over a period of time.

Stage 4

Objective: To become involved in providing a service to the school community.

Purpose

To establish personal relationships with children and significant adults outside of the school situation.

Experiences

1. Volunteer your services for five or six hours a week to a settlement house, the local antipoverty agency, the human relations agency, a public or private housing association, a community health center or any one of the agencies or activities explored in Stage 2.
2. Become a part of a group of community people struggling to develop cohesive action.
3. Organize a new service by suggesting the idea to some parents or other local people and then offering to work with them to develop the idea.
   a. A cooperative food-buying plan.
   b. A cooperative store.
   c. A traveling book store.
   d. Parents group meeting regularly in different homes to discuss and solve school and/or community problems.
   e. An after-school homework center.
   f. A creative dramatics group for parents and children.
   g. A neighborhood school for teaching subjects not taught in public schools.

Experiences of Teachers and Prospective Teachers

Teacher's Reactions to Perception-Map Walk

I walked one child home from school. She lived about five blocks away. It was after school and many children were on the street and so many shouted hello across the street or waved. As they did this, adults on the street nodded or said hello and I seemed to get happier and happier. When I walked back to school actually smiling I began saying hello to people I didn't know. When I first started out I was frightened but it disappeared quickly. I thought I would feel extremely "White" walking in the neighborhood but this feeling seemed to ease up. I was extremely satisfied with the entire thing.

As I walked through the neighborhood I felt somewhat off, as I could feel the adults staring as if to say "Where could she be going?" The children I met, most of whom went to my school, counteracted this feeling somewhat by their pleasant smiles and hellos.

I visited the five and ten cent store and was treated very coolly until attendants heard children say I was a teacher. Then, the salesgirl and I exchanged a few friendly words.

I noticed they had a laundry and a coin-operated dry cleaner right at that corner. I thought about my limited time schedule and how much time it would save if I could use this facility at noontime. I noticed a group of kids just hanging around on various corners and could tell that there is a problem with drop-outs in the neighborhood. I found many small stores which catered to the needs of the people and began to understand why many children have never left their neighborhood.

Since it is an all-white neighborhood and very prejudiced against Blacks, I didn't feel very comfortable at any time. I was very apprehensive about what the people in the neighborhood did and would do. I would, however, do it again, for I imagine it would get easier each time.

I started to enjoy the beautiful clean streets. I wished I lived in the neighborhood. But I realized I could never afford to live so well, and I was envious.

I saw a Black boy pushing a lawn mower and holding a broom. I was stunned to see him in the neighborhood. I thought he came from somewhere else to do the lawns for extra money. As I was wondering where he came from two Black girls walked by. One looked about ten and the other was about seven years old. I smiled at them and they smiled back. But I felt guilty as I realized that they and the boy probably lived in the neighborhood. Although the girls were well dressed and smiled sweetly I felt that they were saying to me through their dress and smile, "See, we can live in a nice neighborhood, too." I'm sure they weren't thinking that but because I felt guilty about my prejudiced observation of the boy, this is the way I interpreted their smiles. I saw that this was an integrated community and felt my own prejudice.

We pass a small playground. Some Black kids are in one corner swinging. As we neared the end of the playground, the far corner on the 72nd St. side, a white kid about seventeen years old jumps out of a car and runs in front of us and up onto a mound of dirt at the corner of the playground. He looks like he's really flying on something. He says, "I own this playground, you gotta pay. You gotta go home and ask your mother for a quarter, cuz I own this playground." We just keep on walking. I'm thinking that if this had happened to me when I was about five to thirteen years old I'd never have gone back to that playground. Even now I'm scared.

We cross over to the project. Here we come across two more kids we teach, sisters. The kids are white. (Who told us there were no white people in the projects?) They're surprised and delighted to see us. Both are good students. The younger offers to bring her mom out. We're pleased. Mrs. Greene comes out and we chat about the weather, how the girls are doing in school, about school in general. As we're leaving, Mrs. Greene says, "It's a nice change to have the teachers coming to visit us instead of us always going to the school to see them." She goes on to say that it's not always too easy to get to school on parent visitation days because she works and has to keep house. I think she speaks for most of our parents . . . for those, at least, who need not fear that teachers are going to tell them how rotten their kids are.

Louise are I are on a kind of high. Without fully verbalizing it to each other, we had been apprehensive about this venture into the unknown. It has been a very positive experience. It's a beautiful spring afternoon. We talk about how it would be if we were familiar sights in the area. We decide that we'll do this again as often as we can for we sense a willing openness in the kids we met. Where there was fear or concern it was generated by the preconception that a teacher in the neighborhood was there for the sole purpose of making a complaint. We knew after today that it wouldn't be difficult to dispel this fear.

A Game for Exploring the Rationale for Community Involvement

A group of teachers or prospective teachers were exploring together the reasons for community involvement. They played this little game to help them discover for themselves the connections between community involvement and more effective teaching:

1. The people sit in a small circle. A receptacle, a basket or pot of some kind, is placed on the floor in the center of the circle.
2. Each person in the circle takes a stack of small cards. On one side of each card everyone writes a behavior problem or a learning difficulty that children in his experience have had.

3. As each card is completed, it is tossed into the receptacle in the middle of the circle.
4. When each one has written as many cards as he can, all cards are picked up, shuffled, and redistributed to the participants.
5. On the other side of each card, each participant writes something he thinks he can learn from parents, from other significant adults in a child's life, from community people, from the neighborhood itself, or from anything *outside the school* that might help the teacher solve the problem of the child whose difficulty is described on the card.
6. Each problem that cannot be solved is thrown back into the receptacle and may be withdrawn by the other participants.
7. The person who has solved the most problems wins the game.
8. The group discusses some of the problems and solutions.
9. It is helpful to list all the problems and solutions and distribute copies to all the participants, so that they may refer to them and make corrections and additions as they continue their work in the community.

A Guide for Developing a Personal Rationale for Community Involvement

Teachers and prospective teachers involved in some aspect of community life at any stage in the plan have explored systematically what was happening to them as people and as professionals. They asked themselves the following questions as they sat in small groups. (However, a teacher working alone can also use the questions as a guide in his own development.)

1. What are you doing in the community? Recount some experiences you have had.
2. How does this activity contribute to your appreciation and understanding of yourself.
   a. What do you find particularly satisfying?
   b. What do you find particularly frustrating?
   c. What are the causes of these feelings?
   d. What have you learned about yourself since you started the activity?

3. How does this activity contribute to your appreciation and understanding of people in the community?
   a. What feelings have people expressed about you directly and indirectly?
   b. What do you think the causes of these feeelings are?
   c. What have you learned about the people in the community?
4. Relate any feeling, experience, or item of new knowledge you have mentioned to an experience you have had in the teaching of children.

A Checklist to Determine the Relationship of the Teacher's Involvement in the Life of the Community to Effective Teaching

This checklist was developed while working with about 150 prospective teachers who were trying to use their community experiences in teaching.

They used this checklist, adding to it as awareness developed in them that teaching effectiveness is *specifically* related to knowledge of and sensitivity to the children's community.

1. Does the teacher understand the language of the children?
2. Do the children understand the language of the teacher?
3. When the teacher uses examples from life to illustrate her ideas, are they examples from *the children's* lives?
4. When the teacher makes her selection of "important" issues to be taken up in class, are they issues that the children perceive as important? How do you know?
5. If the teacher is to make learning pleasurable her methods should include games, for example. Does the teacher utilize games that the children enjoy outside of school?
6. If a child falls asleep in class, how does the teacher deal with the matter? Does she, for example, say to the child, "What's the matter with you; why don't you pay attention?" Or does she also discuss the matter with the child's family, in an attempt to find out what the problem is?
7. Similarly, if a child continually disrupts the class, has the teacher sought help from his mother? Does she know how his mother handles a similar situation, what reasons she sees for her child's behavior?
8. When a child refers to a situation in his own life—for

example, a hoagie shop where his older brother spends his spare time—does the teacher seem to know the shop and some of the events occurring in and around it?

9. Does the teacher refer to recreational and cultural opportunities in the children's neighborhood to excite their interest in using the opportunities?

10. Do the children refer to situations and events that they have shared with the teacher outside the classroom? (Such shared experiences broaden the base of interaction between teacher and child, offering opportunity for communication beyond academic matters. This is especially helpful if the child is having difficulty in school, since it prevents complete collapse of teacher-child contact and supplies the teacher with material for continuing her attempts to make school work meaningful to the child.)

11. Do teacher and children refer to people they have all met in the community? (If the child cannot learn something from the teacher's example, he may be able to learn it from the example of another significant adult in his life. If the teacher knows such an adult, she can refer to him and even call on him to strengthen her classroom teaching.)

12. Does the teacher really appreciate the children whose behaviors seem to violate her own values? (For example, if a child is dirty is the teacher able to accept other things about the child and relate to him positively? If a child uses obscenities, does the teacher respond to what the child is trying to communicate or does she react in a moralistic way to the words? It may be noted that ability to respond to the child in terms of his own strengths and his own needs is a function of knowing the child more intimately than one can in the classroom situation alone.)

13. Does the teacher generalize about "you children" when faced with the behavior of a single child?

14. Does the teacher assume that she knows the causes of a child's behavior when she obviously does not know that child outside the classroom? (Books are filled with causes of the behavior of poor children, Black children, minority children, and so on. Teachers often think they know a particular child because they have read the generalizations.

15. When a child brings food to school, when he talks about certain foods, when there are food sales in the school for special occasions, does the teacher indicate familiarity with and appreciation of foods foreign to his own background?
16. Does the teacher assume that the children are not familiar with certain foods just because they are poor or of another ethnic group? (If the teacher knows the neighborhood, he has seen the varieties of food sold in the stores.)
17. Does the teacher demonstrate more than surface knowledge of ethnic holidays? Does she give the children opportunity to learn about the holidays from each other?
18. Does the teacher demonstrate acceptance of individual behaviors unique to individual families? Is she careful to get her information from the child and his family so that she does not misinterpret them?

Some Things Teachers Have Done as a Direct Result of Their Community Involvement

1. Shown educational films for adults in some neighborhood theatres while children were attending matinées in others.
2. Shown children an entertaining film in class that was geared to their experience and interests to counteract the standard film fare in commercial theatres.
3. Had children do a systematic survey of their community for theatres that do not provide special matinées for children.
4. Had children draw up a petition, engage in selective boycotts, hold demonstrations for children's matinées.
5. Helped children become aware of "economic thrust" (selective buying) in dealing with restaurants that violate health standards, especially those places that young people frequent.
6. Contacted members of gangs in the community and brought them into class to discuss the organization of gangs. This was related to social organizations of groups, clubs, governments, and so on.
7. Ethnic and racial clustering in the area carried over into the school was used to teach the histories and traditions

of different ethnic and racial groups. Children were being encouraged to bring in objects from their own backgrounds to show the others.

8. In one community, mothers staged a sit-in to call attention to inadequate welfare payments. This incident was used as a focus for teaching about civil rights, about alternative ways to change the environment, and about how to make one's self heard in the community.

9. After visiting the police station and learning something about police-community relationships, the teacher had the children learn about policemen and their functions, citizens' rights vis à vis the police, and community feelings about the police.

10. Used community concern about need for a traffic light to teach children how citizens take steps to get what they want.

11. Helped children become aware of the facilities in the community like the Community Health Center. Took children to visit these facilities.

12. An abandoned house in the neighborhood was the focus of a class project to examine the dangers of such a thing, get the broken windows boarded up, and keep an eye out for similar dangers and eyesores.

13. A Black child's family was refused a house in the neighborhood. This became the basis for studying housing discrimination in general and methods of redress.

What Community People Taught the Teachers

A short time, ago, the group of mothers and fathers from communities in the centers of several large cities met to talk about teaching in their schools. Just to get started, they had a brief brainstorming session, in which they tossed out the ideas rapidly without stopping to evaluate them. The topic was "First steps in getting school people involved in the community." This is the list they came up with, and which they set about refining and illustrating:

Get child to invite you home

Publicize community's interest in school people coming in

Hold coffee hours

Set up community centers

Team of parents working with a team of teachers

Make school people feel at ease

Hold block meetings

Stage a demonstration

Kidnap the principal

Have children go on strike

Have cars towed away so they have to come into the community to search for them

Take over the building

Hold new-teacher orientation in the community

Visit the schools to meet school people

Have children list all activities they would like to see teachers participate in

Invite school people to community social

Neighborhood fair

Organize a Parents' Corps

Hospital drive

Teachers attend school board meetings that are held in the community

Have community people tutor teachers

Parent buddy for every teacher

Have your child invite the teacher home

Try to get teacher to invite you home

Community control over school's policies

Have child take teacher to favorite place

Making school people aware of community resources

Hold picnic on school grounds or in park

Set up multi-ethnic group centers to study Spanish, Black history, Indian culture, and so on.

Community teacher assistants

Another group of people from urban, rural, Mexican-American and Appalachian communities, in talking about the Teacher Corps (which emphasizes community involvement in its training program), said about successful Corps programs:

The Corps member makes it a point to get to know each child. He lives in and takes part in the child's community, visits his home, gets to know his parents. He shares with them concerns and interests in the child's education, and encourages their help . . . Above all, he develops a sensitivity to each child's environment and a closeness to each child. He becomes tuned in; the child responds, he learns . . . We cannot understand a person's needs unless we know him. We cannot know him unless we communicate with him. We cannot communicate with him unless we are involved with him. To continue to proceed otherwise is simply to reinforce the same old middle-class failures with "smarter ideas!

8

Evaluating Audiovisual Aids

Description of the Technique

1. Select a film or filmstrip, or play a recording. These aids may have been designed for specific curriculum goals and selected by the school for those special uses, or they may be found in public libraries and other sources of educational materials. Even television shows may be used for this purpose.
2. Tell the pupils briefly what the objective of the producer of the aid was: to teach brotherhood, to discourage drug use, to teach social studies or current problems, and so on.
3. Now, ask them what they would look for in an aid made with this objective in mind. They may suggest anything from good film quality, to up-to-date subject matter; list all of these items on the board where everyone can see them.
4. Show the film (or other aid).
5. Go through each item on the list with the pupils to determine if they have found what they wanted, if the item was, after all, irrelevant, and if there are other criteria that they now think are important.

6. Use the revised criteria to evaluate another audiovisual aid.

Rationale for the Technique

Minimal Selection Necessary

Traditionally, audiovisual aids are selected for school systems on the basis of criteria that a selection committee has in mind. These criteria often are not even spelled out. In addition, the bases for selection are severely circumscribed by the fact that there are not many audiovisual aids available in some curriculum areas, and if teachers are to be encouraged to use such aids it is necessary to purchase whatever is available. The result has been that there are many such aids in almost every school system that are not only virtually useless but that actually teach things we really do not want the children to learn. Instead of trying to evaluate them before we show them, and perhaps being forced to discard them all, with this technique we can show them all and add another dimension to their usefulness.

Develops Critical Viewing, Listening and Reading

The essential aim of the technique is obviously the development of a critical approach to all media. Especially in the areas of race, drugs, and sex, the senses of contemporary populations are so bombarded with material that we are usually manipulated by people whose motives and competencies we do not know. Contributing to the process of freeing young people from ignorance, anxiety and arbitrary controls is the development of skill in analyzing the material with which we are inundated and resisting manipulation by the distributors of that material.

Teachers do recognize this as an educational need, but they often limit the opportunity for critical viewing to materials from outside the classroom, like daily newspapers and television commercials. Rarely do they turn pupils loose (critically speaking) on an audiovisual aid that has been selected by the school for classroom use. We miss a valuable opportunity here to catch the interest of the pupil and motivate him to learn. We can compel him to sit through a film, for example, that is irrelevant, badly acted and dull. But we cannot make him accept its content as valid and useful to him just because we leave no time for criticism. Or we may compel him to sit through a film that is well made, interesting and even exciting, and let him absorb the inaccuracies and the prejudices together with the excitement. Or we may think the film is excellent and never learn that the pupils are far more competent to judge the reality than the film maker was.

Once we open up the classroom and its materials to critical evaluation, we must inevitably come to the textbook, which is the most widely used audiovisual aid. Though we are highly manipulated by the electronic media today, the effect is small compared to the generations of trust we have put in the printed word. If it's in a book it must be right; if it's not in a book it can't be important. Many of us whose mother tongue is English actually believe that the dictionary is the final arbiter in deciding on meanings, even when the words in question are unique to a particular neighborhood and are quite well understood by the people in that neighborhood. We cannot accept that the writers of the dictionary simply have no idea of the real, living meaning of those words.

And just as we attribute a kind of infallibility to books, we have permitted a whole morality to spring up surrounding their physical treatment, as if people who bend the spine of a book are demonstrating a kind of violence. It seems to me that children need not learn to revere books. Rather, they should learn to consume them with circumspection and a cogent awareness that it is people who write books, and people are often prejudiced, ignorant, vicious, and mistaken, as well as authoritative, accurate and honest. Exposing a book to critical analysis while using it as a school text may very well create interest in it when uncritical reading, outlining, and memorizing never will.

Experiences in Using the Technique

Second Grade

One teacher tells of an interesting experience she had in the use of an audiovisual aid. During Dental Health Week she was teaching a series of lessons for her second-graders on care of the teeth. The oral hygienist of the school district had recommended a film that was suitable for this purpose. The district had bought it and was making it available to all the teachers. In encouraging the teachers to set aside time for teaching about care of the teeth, the hygienist enthusiastically reported that all the children who saw the film loved it, and really learned the tooth-care lesson. The teacher ordered the film from the district, pleased to have additional assistance in teaching a subject in which she felt no great proficiency.

Characteristically, the film was delivered to the classroom somewhat later in the day than it was promised for and there was no time for her to preview it before showing it to the children. With confidence in her ability to use it to advantage without preparation, she threaded it into the waiting projector, darkened the room, and started it.

What the hygienist had said was true: The children loved the film! The animated sequences demonstrated amusingly and clearly that if teeth were not cared for the enemy (the little black characters) would attack the good guys (the white characters). However, since virtue always triumphs, the good white characters would be saved by other whites riding in on white horses and scattering the blacks out of the picture.

Not only were the children absorbed and interested, so was the teacher. By the time she realized the implications of what they were seeing, it would have been unwise to stop the film. The outcry would have been loud and anguished, and justifiably so. An arbitrary, "We won't watch any more of this," would have reinforced the attractiveness of the film and done nothing to ameliorate harmful effects. What the children would have learned, perhaps, was that arbitrary authority inevitably prevails.

So, thinking fast on her feet, she decided to lead the children in an evaluative analysis of what they had just seen. "What are the things you liked about the movie?" she asked. The children made it clear that what they enjoyed most was the conflict, with the good guys triumphing over the bad guys. In a variation on this response, one child engaged another in an exuberant acting out of the conflict, shouting, "You're the black devil, I'm the white tooth. Charge!!"

"The film showed Black people are the enemy," the teacher said mildly, with a hint of a question in her voice.

"Yes," said one child.

"No," said another. "It was Black *teeth*."

"It was not," said a third. "It was cavities."

"They looked like little people," said one child musingly. "Little Black people."

"Black people aren't bad."

"Black teeth are."

"People aren't teeth."

"Some Black people fight."

"Some white people fight too."

And they were off on a discussion of race relations in the course of which the teacher was able to diagnose stereotypic thinking, fears and anxieties surrounding race, and hostilities toward people of other races.

Somewhere in the course of the discussion the teacher asked, "What did the movie teach you about teeth?" The group's answer was a casual and nonspecific, "You should take care of your teeth." In a calmer moment, the teacher considered the validity of the film in terms of its stated objective: to teach children how to care for their teeth. It apparently offered them little on this but a vague exhortation, but it left them with a clear impression that the Blacks must be vanquished. Bringing this impression up to a verbal level and examining it helped insulate the children against uncritical reinforcement of racial bias, and set them on the road to questioning what they experience.

Policemen

I remember showing a film on race relations to several groups of policemen. At a number of identical points during the film each group laughed. During the discussions they reacted to my probing questions about the ideas on race that were presented in the film in a rather desultory manner. I felt strong resistance to those ideas and a sort of stiff-jawed determination to keep the discussion at a minimal level of participation. But the film was being discussed at some length after class. The subject of discussion however was not race relations! Apparently, what seemed to have made the greatest impact were the outmoded clothes and hair fashions and an Edsel car that kept reappearing in scene after scene. It seemed to me afterwards that if the men had been encouraged to view the film critically in class, they might have laughed openly at the anachronisms and then more freely and comfortably turned to the intergroup ideas, instead of resisting them out of hand in such a way that I could not establish communication about them.

Teen-agers

A counselor announced to a class of teen-agers that he had obtained a good educational tape on drug abuse prepared by a physician. The tape, he said, really gave the facts on drugs, pulling no punches and the students were well advised to heed its message. The speaker on the tape went down the usual list of horror stories, prohibitions and warnings and ended by exhorting his listeners to stay "clean" and "decent" for the sake of their families as well as for their own futures. The youngsters listened to the tape in stony silence. When it ended, the counselor asked rhetorically, "Wasn't that great? There's a lot to think about there!" And he dismissed the students, with their questions, their doubts, their fears and their convictions (about all of which he had no inkling) unanswered, undealt with, and intact.

Elementary School Children

A recent *Punch* cartoon seems so clearly to illustrate the essential ideas that have taken me so many words to explain. A group of children are filing into a room. Through the door, an adult (presumably the teacher) is setting up a film projector. The children are apparently somewhat less than delighted with what they know is about to happen, and one child has put the prevailing feeling into words. "Not sex again!" he moans.

Can it be that fourth-graders are not interested in the subject of sex? Or is it more likely that the films they are shown simply do not address themselves to their concerns, and in ways that they understand and appreciate? But the real point is that the teacher continues to show the films, unaware of the children's feelings and thoughts.

Sample Evaluative Criteria

Several months ago, a group of teaching supervisors gathered for a workshop in race relations education. Before viewing one of the films on intergroup education they listed a number of qualifications that such a film should have. A good intergroup education film, they said,

1. Gives accurate information.
2. Provokes thought about intergroup relations.
3. Is correlated with current happenings.
4. Stimulates other activities.

After seeing the film and discussing its effect on them and its possible effect on children, they revised their criteria to include areas that had not occurred to them. They added that it

5. Stirs up feelings about intergroup relations and conveys the feelings of the people pictured in the aid.
6. Is relevant to children's diagnosed needs in intergroup relations:
   a. Should teach to changing patterns of behavior
   b. Should teach to changing attitudes
7. Does not preach.

They also revised Item 1 in their first list. After seeing the film they realized that an aid that presented inaccurate data could be valuable too if the youngsters were led to check out the accuracy of *all* information presented to them. So the first criterion was changed to: The information presented need not be accurate.

They changed Item 3 to read: Is correlated with current happenings and related to intergroup relations in the everyday environment. And then, to the final list of seven criteria they added a footnote: If the audiovisual aid does not meet these criteria, it may still be used as evidence of an unfulfilled need in the area of education.

You will note that the opportunity for critical evaluation provided for the supervisors encouraged them to go beyond the rather academic criteria in the first list and begin to consider the importance of feelings, the value of learning by discovery and the educational limitations of exhortation. Subsequently some of these supervisors exposed groups of children to the technique and were gratified that the children demonstrated similar evidences of expanded awareness and sensitivity. They were even more pleased that the children came up with several criteria that they had never thought of. One was: Indicates clearly if the events described are realistic or idealistic. Here the students were conveying the idea that the producer of an aid might easily, in his eagerness to make a point, overstate his case. However they were reluctant to imply that this would be lying: They chalked it up to idealism and determined to be wary of its undue influence on them.

The following criteria were developed by ninth-grade pupils before and after viewing a set of transparencies on sex education:

Before

Should give information.
Should be interesting.
Should answer practical questions.
Should deal with the real world.

After

Should protray people, not just cells and processes.
Should answer practical questions.
Should deal with the world today, not fifty years ago.
Should give young people's point of view, not just adults'.
Should give many points of view.
Should give facts, not moralize.

General Educational Effects of Involvement in the Technique

Children taught to react critically to audiovisual materials are more likely to develop a healthy skepticism toward what is presented for their consumption. A generation of youngsters, cajoled into demanding breakfast foods because a clown on TV says he loves them or because the cereal box contains toys, can begin to question the motives of the purveyors of such advertisements and temptations. Similarily children are fed on the pap of a national "hero" who never told lies. Or they are encouraged to venerate a "great man" who devoted his life to a total commitment to world government (while he actively encouraged racism at home). The children can begin to see these historical figures as real and imperfect people, for realistic critical analysis becomes a way of life for those who learn it. Citizens who see men in public office realistically are not so easily swayed by electioneering slogans or appeals to total order. They see that total order is as unrealistic as total perfection. Consequently, their expectations do not lead them into chasms of disappointment and disillusion that have paralyzed so many of us into abandoning efforts at social change.

We do much, especially in the social studies, to help teachers learn the "inquiry method" of teaching. hoping that this will encourage in children just this kind of healthy skepticism and active participation in the learning process. But usually we confine the inquiry method to small cognitive areas, saying in effect, "Inquiry method will be used during the fourth period social studies lesson when we are studying about the westward expansion in the United States." But the children are rarely encouraged to use the inquiry method in other areas of relationship with teachers. By implication we teach them that, "When *I* tell you something, *that is gospel*; when I bring in someone to speak about drugs or show you a film on sex, just learn it; when I institute a mode of classroom management, then just live by it. After all, there are *some* things you must take on faith!"

But the responsible citizen questions everything. He does not, of course, limit his activity to questioning. If his skepticism is really healthy and not merely nihilistic, he takes the next step after questioning: He proceeds to check out the qualifications of authorities, examine the motives of speakers, and double-check the scientific validity of data. In sum, he refuses to take a passive role in his own education or in other facets of his life.

The implications for the teacher who encourages this process are serious. He will no longer be able to keep students quietly in their seats for hours while they listen to his words. He will no longer be able to assign homework that follows traditional formulas. He will, in other words, be compelled to reliquish his traditional role of disseminator of information and supervisor of classroom order, and become himself a leader in the process of questioning, searching, and checking.

9

Exercises in Selective Perception

Rationale for the Technique

Precipitating Self-Knowledge

Exercises in selective perception constitute an exciting educational technique. Such exercises are simple to use and even fun for the participants. Not inconsequentially, the procedure may also be connected to some real experiences of pupils, for the technique is very much like a game most children play. The major difference is that, though children delight in trapping each other in obvious errors as a whispered message changes between the first whisperer and the fifth or sixth, they do not usually connect the process of the game with the spread of rumor or the perpetuation of prejudice.

It is a most effective learning situation when the pupil suddenly sees something about himself and his own behavior that he has never before been aware of. The teacher may, over and over again, maintain that people see what they expect to see, distort reality, and interpret a situation in terms of their fears, hostilities and anxieties. But until the pupil actually finds himself doing all these things, the information is simply not useful. The exercises in selective perception are designed to do just this: To put the student into a situation where he can actually experience his own propensity for filtering data through his own unique perceptions. When he compares what he perceives with what other people perceive, he begins to know something about himself he probably never knew before.

The person who says he has no racial prejudice, that he never even "sees" the race of a person, can quickly and dramatically discover that he does see race: That race influences what he thinks of people and what he expects of them. When he looks at a picture in which a white man holds a tool of some kind and describes it as a Black man holding a razor, then he gets some indication that his words and his perceptions do not always match.

Lack of self-knowledge and ignorance of the process of selective perception actually help to reinforce a person's prejudices. If he "sees" only what he expects and needs to see, then each experience of "seeing" merely provides corroborative evidence that the stereotype is not a lie at all. I expect Black men to commit crimes; I see a Black man; he looks suspicious to me; I run; I am sure that if I had not run he would have done something criminal to me. So I become my own agent for providing the evidence that convinces me that I was right all along!

The person who has learned to see Black people as menacing or long-haired people as immoral finds ample evidence for persisting in his prejudicial thinking. He expects that long-haired people will be immoral, so he sees "proof" of immorality in everything they do —a casual word, an arm around someone, a communal living situation. When someone with long hair actually is found to have done something immoral—like the Manson killings—this is merely used as corroborative evidence of what the individual "knew" all along.

Among policemen, for example, we see this process operating with tragic consequences. Many of them start out with the conviction that Black people are more inclined to criminality than are whites. Consequently, they are more suspicious when they see a Black person than when they see a white person in the same situation. They actually "see" a Black person trying to hide something, or trying to hide himself, or having a bulge in his pocket that means a weapon. Therefore Black people—especially Black men—are more often stopped for questioning or frisking. When this happens very often, they become angry at the injustice and begin to resist the questioning and frisking, and arguments and fights erupt between policemen and Black citizens. The result is that many Black men get police records for assault and battery on an officer and for resisting arrest. It is a rare magistrate who questions closely to determine what crime brought the policeman on the scene and resulted in the attempt to make an arrest. The "crime" for which the person is charged occurs after the policeman arrives on the scene!

Thus it is difficult for Black men in large cities to grow to maturity without having a police record. This fact in turn reinforces the expectations of people who see Blacks as criminals. The number of lives damaged by these errors in perception, translated into discriminatory behavior, is incalculable.

An individual who sees himself as open and free of bigotry needs to experience the inconsistencies in his awareness of himself. Thus, when he realizes that he has attributed pro-draft sentiments to everyone over thirty, it may be the beginning of self-knowledge.

Similarly, the adult who "loves" children yet sees them also as not to be trusted with information or self-determination needs to be confronted with the severe limits of his "love."

It is only a part of the problem that we stereotype each other, reject each other, and interfere with each other's growth. The irony of our lives is that we usually are not aware of what we are doing. It is the other guy who is prejudiced, the foreigner who wants to rule the world. We always want peace, we love our neighbors, and we do only what we would have others do to us. Getting through this smokescreen to more accurate knowledge of one's self is probably the most difficult job a person has in the education of himself. It is truly gratifying to see the looks of surprise and chagrin on the faces of the participants in these exercises in selective perception when they suddenly see themselves more clearly.

Self-Knowledge Aids Learning

When a person thinks he knows his own motives, thinks he sees things clearly and accurately, and thinks his conclusions are based on objective examination of data, his further learning is obviously handicapped. What motivation can he have to examine new data or question his own perception of data if he has no doubts about what he already "knows?" These exercises lead him easily into experiences that reveal his need for further learning to *himself.* There is no more effective motivational force than this kind of revelation.

Nor does such self-knowledge influence only affective areas of learning. Even the cognitive aspects of education may be touched by awareness of one's own errors of perception. If a Black student believes that all white people discriminate against Black students, will he feel it worthwhile to make an effort in a white teacher's mathematics class? If a middle-aged teacher thinks young people who have long hair and wear ragged jeans are probably taking drugs, will he engage such a youngster in serious discussion of social issues, giving him credit for earnest concern and a legitimate point of view? If a little boy thinks little girls are all silly, will he work constructively in a science class with the girl next to him?

Self-Knowledge Reduces Victimization

Though the exercises in themselves clearly show the participants that there are universal pitfalls in perception and communication, it is not always so clear how these pitfalls affect their own everyday lives. For example, many of us who have worked in elementary schools have experienced a curious phenomenon: Suddenly, in the middle of an afternoon, fear sweeps through the school. Children's eyes grow big with anxiety; there are whispers about "the green lady" who is coming to get someone or the crooked man who is coming to cut off all the girls' hair. The fear grows and becomes palpable. Some children begin to cry, some sound almost hysterical. Long before dismissal time worried mothers are congregating at the doors of the school to make sure their children are safe, though it is never clear how the news of what is happening reaches them. (I have always thought that often one child manages to escape home, running from the danger he perceives.) The school literally stops functioning for that day, and it is not for several days afterward that routine settles down to normal again.

Who knows from exactly what source this rumor springs? It may be from the endless list of child fears that are never dealt with openly, the myriad anxieties that grow from the meaningful looks

and fearful avoidances of adults, out of which comes this an-
thropomorphic menace. But, just as little is done in school to deal
with the *nameless* anxieties, nothing is done about the fear that has
become the "green lady."

If the children were aware of the process that is going on in the
spread of the rumor, the distortions that occur and the emotions
that are attached to them, they would not be so vulnerable to its
effects. They would know that they themselves distorted stories in
the telling and retelling, and they might stop to ask someone who
told them a story, "How do you know this? Who told you? Who told
him? Let's ask someone who is in a position *really* to know." In
addition, they may be moved to stop retelling the story and so stop
the spread of fear and hysteria.

As a society, we are coming to some awareness of our limitations of perception. In a number of cities we have actually established rumor control centers to help ourselves. At any hour of the
day or night a citizen may, instead of retelling a horror story he has
just heard, call rumor control and have it checked out. Who knows
how many hysterical outbursts of violence have been headed off this
way?

Even little children are more amenable to learning from their
own experiences than they are to exhortation. Telling someone who
is frightened out of his wits that there is nothing to worry about is,
to say the least, not very useful. Better to prepare children for
assaults on their senses than demand that they be sensible when
they have already lost control.

Description of the Technique

An Exercise in Selective Perception

The class is seated in a large semicircle. At the open end is a
screen. An overhead projector is set up.

TEACHER: When we see something happening or when we are
told about an incident, we filter what we see or hear
through our own beliefs and feelings. What we finally
believe we saw or heard may be quite different from
what actually happened. Instead of talking about this,

	let's try a little experiment to check it out.

let's try a little experiment to check it out.

Is there anyone here who, when he sees an incident, can tell pretty well what happened?

CLASS: *(Sheepish smiles, a giggle or two, and studious avoidance of the teacher's eye!)*

TEACHER: Oh, come on. Nothing is going to happen to you! And nobody expects you to remember perfectly. Just so you have an idea of what happened when you see something.

STUDENT 1:   I'll try.

TEACHER: Good!

Now—we need some people who know what they hear when somebody tells them something. Five people.

CLASS: *(Laughs. Murmurs of "What are we gonna hear? Hear what?")*

STUDENT 2:   I guess I can hear all right.

TEACHER: Great! Who else? Come on, we can't do this unless we get volunteers.

STUDENT 3:   Okay, I'm game.

STUDENT 4:   Me too.

TEACHER: You and you. *(To students 5 and 6 who are smiling and shrugging as if they are not averse to being one of the group.)* Now, will the six of you please leave.

CLASS: *(Laughter)*

TEACHER: Just step outside for a few minutes. We'll call you in when we're ready.

(To the rest of the class) I'm going to flash a picture on the screen. I want you to say what you see in the picture.

(Flashes picture.) What do you see?

STUDENT A: It looks like a riot.

STUDENT B: No it doesn't. It's just a crowd of people.

STUDENT A: They look angry. Look at them crowded up against that police barricade.

STUDENT C: What barricade? That's just a fence around the building.

TEACHER: Do you see what's happening? You're all looking at the same scene, but you're seeing different things.

STUDENT A: Which one of us is right?

TEACHER: I don't know. I see the same picture you're looking at; I don't know any more than you do.

STUDENT D: That cop with the bull horn seems to be warning them. There must be something going on.

STUDENT C: That's not a cop. He looks like a guard or a tour-guide or something.

TEACHER: What else do you see?

STUDENT E: It's evening.

STUDENT F: It's summer; they're not wearing coats.

TEACHER: All right. Now I'm going to call back the person who said he could see pretty well. We'll show him the picture and then we'll ask him to tell the next person what he saw. That person will tell the next one, and so on. We'll be able to hear how the scene changes as it goes from person to person.

STUDENT C: Oh, I know this! We used to play this when we were kids! We called it Telephone.

STUDENT D: We call it Whispering Down the Lane!

TEACHER: That's right. Let's try it now. Remember, we've got to be absolutely quiet while they do this. If you laugh when someone changes the story, you'll give it away; he'll backtrack and make a correction. So be very still. You can take notes on the changes so you can remember them.

(Calls in the "seeing" person.)

Stand so that you can see the screen. We're going to show you a picture. You may look at it for as long as you like, then we'll take it off, and we'll call in the next person. You will tell that person what you saw happening in the picture. Okay?

STUDENT 1: Okay.

(Teacher flashes picture on screen. Student 1 takes about two minutes to look at it.)

STUDENT 1: *(Turns to teacher, smiling.)*

TEACHER: Finished?

STUDENT 1: I guess so.

(Teacher takes picture off and goes to door.)

TEACHER: Next person. Will you come in, please? Now, just stand up there. (Motions Student 2 to stand in open part of semi-circle about three feet from Student 1.*

(The procedure continues until the last person comes into the room.)

TEACHER: *(To Student 6)* He (Student 5) has just had a happening described to him. He will tell you what he heard. You listen carefully, don't ask any questions. Then we'll ask you to tell the class what you heard.

(When Student 6 completes his telling of the incident, the teacher thanks him and asks him to take his seat. Then she turns expectantly to the class.)

TEACHER: Well, what happened?

STUDENT A: The details got fewer and fewer.

TEACHER: Yes, that often happens when this is done in front of an audience. Maybe people are a little cautious about making mistakes, so they just leave out items.

STUDENT B: Jim changed the . . .

TEACHER: Let's not bother to identify who did what. Just stay with the changes.

STUDENT B: The bullhorn became an instrument.

STUDENT C: It sounded almost as if people were being beaten.

STUDENT H: There's been so much in the news about police beating people, we just expected it.

STUDENT 4: Can we see the picture?

TEACHER: Oh yes. When we've talked a little more about what happened.

(Discussion of distortions and omissions continues.)

TEACHER: *(When all the changes have been identified and there is a lull.)* Would those of you who were outside like to see the picture?

(Flashes it on the screen.)

Does it look anything like what you thought it would?

STUDENT 2: No!

---

*The idea is to have the students far enough from each other so they will have to speak loudly enough for the rest of the class to hear them.

Student 3: I thought it was happening in a building!

Student 5: If I could have asked questions I would have got it right. I just didn't hear what he said.

Teacher: Yes, that's probably true to some extent. Asking questions, clarifying and so on can reduce the margin of error. However, it often introduces additional errors because we continue the distortion as we continue to talk.

Student G: The trouble is we don't really listen.

Teacher: Now that you know the pitfalls, would you like to try it again with another picture?

Class: (Chorus of yes, yes, yes.)

(This time six volunteers quickly come forward. This is fun! The exercise is repeated with the new picture. This time the teacher does not give each person the directions, since they already know the procedure.)

Teacher: Isn't that interesting? You knew the pitfalls and you were very careful, but the distortions still occurred! Does this give you any ideas?

Student A: I'll never believe anything anyone tells me again!

Class: *(Laughter.)*

Student C: Don't believe anything you hear and only half of what you see.

Student H: You certainly have to be careful about spreading rumors!

Student F: What about news reporters—they must do some of this too!

Student E: The same thing happens if you have long hair. Police and people expect you to be into drugs and things—and they don't believe you if you say you're not.

(The discussion continues with the sharing of personal experiences with selective perception.)

Criteria for Selecting Pictures

The Anti-Defamation League provides four frames on a film strip, each frame a cartoon drawing of an action scene with people of various groups participating in activities that lend themselves to subjective interpretation *(The Rumor Clinic).* Though these pictures are excellent for the exercise, the teacher need not limit himself to using only these. As a matter of fact, it is of value to find other pictures that are, perhaps, more up-to-date in the way people are dressed and more meaningful in terms of current events. The pictures must, however, contain certain things before they can be useful:

1. They must have people of at least two identifiable racial, ethnic, age, sex or other social groups.

2. The people must be engaged in activity that can be understood in a number of different ways. That is, it cannot be indisputably clear that the people are doing something that everyone can agree on.

3. If the possibility of agreement is great, the chances are that the details of the picture are so free of emotional implications that objectivity is easy to maintain. So, aside from the inclusion of individuals from different groups—which in itself has emotional implications for most Americans—the activities they are engaged in should also lend themselves to emotional interpretation.

4. It facilitates the process if there are items in the picture that are more prominent than other items. Thus, the viewers are prompted to differentiate in perception—sometimes on no other basis than prominence. It is possible that the emphasis that some people put on often insignificant background details is a function of the need to play it safe. That is, aware of the pitfalls of "misinterpreting" a picture with racial implications, they make a point of repeating the nonracial background details, and so minimize the possibility of revealing prejudice.

5. If the picture is too obviously out of date, this tends to distract the viewer and seems to help him veer away from revealing any attitudes about current life. The picture takes on a "period" atmosphere that enables him to see it from the perspective of distance and time, and whatever feeings he may have about race, for example, are filtered through this perspective.

6. Sometimes it is difficult to find just exactly the right kind of picture for these exercises. One teacher solved this

problem in a rather interesting way: he cut parts from different pictures and put them together into a suitable scene. For example, he put a cut-out picture of a Black man into a street scene where all the people were white. Though the montage was not as technically perfect as a photograph, the children did not seem to mind the imperfection and the exercise was successfully concluded.

An Experience in Using the Technique

I cannot help adding another experience I had recently with this technique. In a session with parents and teachers of Ute Indian children in the southwest, I wondered how I could get the six Ute women in the group to participate. (As is usually the case, the teachers were all Anglos, and they had no trouble taking an active part in the discussions on the education of Ute children.) I decided to try the exercise in selective perception, and had six volunteers— all Anglos—repeat a story and observe the distortions that occurred. At one point I heard one Ute women whisper to another that if they put in some Ute words, then there would really be distortion, because the Anglos would not understand the meanings. I leaned close to the whisperers and said it would be fun to try.

The upshot was that the six Ute women did the whole experiment in Ute, with the last person translating the final version of the story into English. And the value of the lesson could be seen on the faces of the teachers, who watched and listened to the laughing, vocal, perceptive Ute women whom they had viewed as characteristically silent, uncommunicative and even unperceptive! *That* was a "teachable moment" I had pounced upon—and that I shall never forget.

10

Instituting Change

Rationale for the Techniques

Values and Teaching*

A curious phenomenon may be observed among young teachers these days. Whenever anyone expresses a judgment about anything, they object half humorously by announcing, "That's a value judgment!" It is as if they are reacting against the endless string of teacher evaluations behind them, the continuing shower of "That's right," "That's wrong," "That's good," "That's bad." They seem to feel that any expression of values, any open evaluative stand on an issue is somehow undesirable. It is time to adjust the swing of the pendulum somewhat and examine again the whole idea of identifying, clarifying and expressing values.

Certainly what we teachers do not want to do is impose our values on our students. We have made decisions in our own lives

*See Raths, Harmin, and Simon, *Values and Teaching* (Columbus: Charles E. Merrill Books, Inc., 1966) for specific techniques in valuing.

thal seemed best for us. But the world changes, new needs become apparent, old solutions prove ineffective, and we must leave young people free to determine the appropriateness of existing values for themselves and even arrive at new ones we may ourselves reject. We may argue that some values are eternal and that there are universal verities that we must transmit to the next generation. We may believe this and we may even announce our beliefs to our young people, but our power to make *them* believe as we do is limited by their perception of reality. The best we can do is to free them to see the real world, free them to accept themselves and each other, and then trust them to live by their own values.

This is not to say that teachers should not make their own values known to students. On the contrary, students are entitled to know where we stand, so that they may know the roots of our teachings. If we are really to permit them to view authority with a healthy skepticism then we must let them see that the attitudes and behaviors of authorities are rooted in values. But this is a very difficult part of the teacher's job: to make her values explicit without coercing her students to adopt those values. Given the power of the teacher to pass or fail, to mark test answers right or wrong, it is a fine line we walk between openness and coercion.

Traditionally, we have sought to inculcate in children the values that we ourselves hold. We have bolstered this goal by defining it as a philosophical position: "The function of the schools is to hand down the culture of the society." Actually, this goal has been only partially achieved in the past. And in the last five years or so, it becomes abundantly clear that the young are increasingly repudiating the values that are a part of our culture. There have been a number of consequences of this repudiation:

1. The gap between the children and their teachers has widened so greatly that children are dropping out of school at the rate of 50 percent in some areas.
2. Many of the values adopted by young people are not so much valued as they are weapons to be used against constricting adults who are deaf to the voices of the young.
3. Large numbers of young people are caught in the confusion of conflicting values. They feel frightened and lost

and do not know how to sort out what is happening and find some consistent rationale for their own choices.

Knowing the Issues

All of the techniques described in this book are designed to help people explore the human issues of our time and begin to discover where they stand on those issues. Whereas the strategies permit the teacher to exercise initiative in bringing issues to the students' attention, all the strategies encourage the gathering of information, the proliferation of personal experiences, the free expression of feelings and the practicing of new behaviors. Inevitably, knowledge about the issues is accumulated, whether it is out in the community, within the school building, or in the classroom among peers.

Exploring Consequences of Behavior

While students are learning new things they are also, in relative safety, exploring the consequences of alternative solutions to problems. Partly they do this in role-playing. But also when they are encouraged to express their ideas and feelings freely, they are learning something about how others respond to such expressions in the classroom that offers them some measure of protection. Even when they are working out in the community, they are still viewed as children, pupils, and students, and the errors they make in their interpersonal relations may be examined in the calm of the educational setting.

Taking a Stand

Involved as the students become in working with new people, exploring alternative behaviors in role-playing, and sharing points of view on race, on drugs, and on sex, they inevitably are moved to take a public stand on the issues. Though they do this quite naturally as the interaction and the situations move them, it is often clear to the teacher that their points of view need clarification and consistency.

Values, I think, are identifiable insofar as they precipitate certain behaviors. In controversial issues, the chosen behaviors of a society are the critical factors influencing change or the lack of it. If social change is to be progressive and rational and as orderly as is possible with change, it needs a firm undergirding of clear and consistent personal values that people openly express. This has not been our condition as a nation. We have as a nation advanced one set of values and as individuals owned up to a conflicting set. This has certainly been true in the areas of race and sex. Even in the use of drugs the conflict and inconsistency in values has been apparent: Witness the confusion in values surrounding the use of various drugs like alcohol, marijuana and tranquilizers.

So if education is to encourage needed social change, the generation of people in the process of being educated need serious and specific assistance in clarifying their values and checking them for consistency. Then they need to be helped to develop skills for acting on those values.

Acting on Values: Effecting Change

As Raths, Harmin and Simon point out, values are personal things, prized and cherished by their holders. If they are really prized, then the action that naturally grows out of them is eagerly engaged in. There comes a time, then, when it is necessary to fish or cut bait. That is, one must engage in action based on those values or admit that the expressed values are merely a verbal facade covering one's truly cherished values.

Also, one may engage forever in role-playing and other simulation exercises and not be moved to take a first step in real life. It is safe in the shelter of the teaching situation where the skills and knowledge are developed in simulation. But when pupils begin to take action to change that classroom where they have been learning to effect change, the dangers become apparent. The teacher may suddenly realize, with full force, the implications of freeing pupils, for they begin to use their freedom to assume a larger measure of control over their own lives *in the classroom!* And when they branch out to work to make changes in the school, then the threat that their freedom represents can become almost untenable—because there are colleagues and supervisors and principals with whom the teacher must contend.

Here is where the teacher's values come into play! Does he

really value knowledgeable and responsible freedom in young people (or in teachers, if he is an educator of teachers)? If he does, then his action cannot be limited to educating his students for freedom in some theoretical sense. This is a contradiction in terms. He must complete the process of educating by offering opportunities for students to use their freedom to change their own lives.

As teachers and as adults, we may very well be disturbed by those changes insofar as they affect us. We may have to make significant adjustments in our own professional behavior to accommodate them. We may have to defend our philosophy of teaching rather desperately when the changes touch school administrators and other adults

But this is the nature of teaching; it is what makes teaching the most exciting, dynamic and terrifying of professions! If we really do the job as it should be done, we will educate a new generation that will scare the wits out of us with their fantastically new ideas, their great courage, and their new modes of life. It is a big risk that we take—this educating people to be free! Perhaps before you take a step you ought to try the following technique on yourself.

Description of the Techniques

The Value Sheet*

The value sheet in a very simple technique that offers opportunity to identify the various points of view on a single issue and then decide which point of view is one's own. It requires only that the teacher be aware of all the points of view that are held and to be careful that, in listing those points of view, she does not inadvertently make out a better case for the statement that represents her own opinion.

The pupils merely follow the directions on the value sheet. When they have finished, the teacher may ask them to share their choices, *if they wish*, either in small groups or with the whole class. Or the teacher may merely say, "Perhaps you'll want to think about this some more," and end the session on that note.

*Adapted from Raths, Harmin and Simon, *op. cit.*

An interesting lesson can be based on a value sheet by letting people determine what the consequences of each value might be to the individual and to the group holding the value. In small groups, students might all pretend to hold one of the views and decide very specifically and in great detail how they would live one day in their lives based on this value. They would write their journey from getting up in the morning, to relationships with each member of the family, to behavior on the way to school, to activities in school, after school, on the way home, at dinner, on dates, and so on. The frame of reference for each decision made in the course of the hypothetical day would be the value under discussion.

This kind of exercise helps the individual clarify a point of view for himself, for he is better able to make a realistic decision about where he stands when he has considered what he is committed to *do* as a result of his point of view.

The value sheets may be used partly for diagnostic purposes. If the teacher wants to collect the sheets after the pupils have indicated their choices, she should tell them so in advance so that they may take steps to insure anonymity if they wish. Without names on the sheets, it is possible to discover how *the class* stands on an issue. Individual stands are revealed when individuals are moved to do so voluntarily.

With very young children who cannot read or write, the value sheet may still be used. For example, after several lessons on the topic, the class may be led to identify the range of points of view in their own words. These points of view are written by the teacher, each one on a sheet of experience chart paper. This is the kind of thing that primary teachers often do: the children tell their experiences and the teacher writes them down on the chart paper. The interesting thing is that even nonreaders are able to recognize their own words on the charts.

When the charts, each with a point of view written on it, are all ranged on the walls, children may be encouraged to decide which point of view they agree with. Some may want to write their names or initials on the chart of their choice. Others may prefer to keep their choices to themselves, others may want to discuss their choices with one or two classmates. Even with very small children, the teacher may lead an examination of the consequences of living by each value.

Other interesting adaptations of the value sheet may be seen in the following examples.

Sample Value Sheets

ON FREEDOM IN THE CLASSROOM: FOR TEACHERS

Choose from the statements below one that best describes how you feel. Combine them in any way, omit parts that do not apply, and add in your own words whatever may be missing. The important thing is that when you are finished you should be able to say about your statement, "This is how I feel."

1. The trouble with today's younger generation is that it has been reared in too permissive an atmosphere. Young people have been permitted to do just about as they please, and that is the reason for all the drug abuse, sexual promiscuity and disorder. It is time for adults to pull in the reins and start setting limits again, and the classroom is a good place to make it clear what those limits are.

2. Freedom is a way of life that few people have learned adequately. To live free requires a positive, realistic self-concept, a mind not afraid to inquire and discover, courage to change with new knowledge and new conditions, and skills for learning interacting and problem-solving. A person in the process of being really educated is in the process of learning to be free.

3. Freedom is important, but youngsters are not capable of using it wisely. When we have given them all they need at home and in school, then will be the time for them to exercise their freedom.

4. Freedom carries with it responsibilities. When young people prove that they are willing to assume their responsibilities, then they will be entitled to freedom. While they are in school is no time to experiment with freedom; this is the time for teachers to teach them their responsibilities.

5. The teacher is the authority in the classroom by virtue of her training and maturity. To suggest that students should be free to

say what they should learn and how they should be taught is silly. This kind of thing leads only to disorder and a breakdown of authority. Young people should learn to respect the authority of the teacher, and this is done by maintaining order and seeing to it that a calm atmosphere for learning is established in the classroom.

ON STUDENT SELF-GOVERNMENT: FOR HIGH SCHOOL STUDENTS

Below are several paragraphs relating to one issue. Select the paragraph that comes closest to your own position and change the wording in it until it represents your thinking as exactly as possible. Or you may write a new position if none of the ones listed is close to the one you prefer. The idea is to get a statement about which you can say, "This is how I stand."

1. High school students really do not have the ability to make decisions concerning school management, teaching quality, curriculum and discipline. There is no point adding to the chaos in the schools by letting students have a direct part in such decisions. Anyhow, the job of students is to learn what they are taught. This is enough to keep them occupied.

2. High school students are in the process of growing up. They are naturally rebellious—often without knowing just what they are rebelling about. They need the opportunity to express their point of view about curriculum and discipline. Teachers and administrators should listen to their opinions before they make the final decisions.

3. There is no way of becoming an effective citizen in a democracy without real experience functioning in a democratic situation. School government—with real powers and responsibilities—can be the stepping stone to local and national government. Part of the value of participation in democratic school government is that it presents opportunity for testing ideas and actions in a relatively safe environment, in which actively-involved adults are always

present with help, advice and rescue. The argument that all students do not become involved is not valid for rejecting the value of student government: a) all citizens do not get involved in the civil governments; b) perhaps if young people developed interest and skills in self-government, they would be more active citizens when they left school.

4. High school students know when teaching is boring or meaningless to them. They should participate directly in making decisions regarding the evaluation of teaching and of curriculum. Students also know much about why some students become discipline problems, and their knowledge should be part of the basis on which decisions are made concerning discipline.

5. High school students know better what they need than adults do. They know what constitutes good teaching, they know what the effects of discipline are, and they should be permitted to make their own decisions in these areas.

ON TEACHING RACE RELATIONS: FOR TEACHERS AND PROSPECTIVE TEACHERS

Below are several paragraphs relating to one issue. Select the paragraph that comes closest to your own position and change the wording in it until it represents your thinking as exactly as possible. Or you may write a new position if none of the ones listed is close to the one you prefer. The idea is to get a statement about which you can say, "This is where I now stand."

A useful way to decide between alternatives is to identify the *consequences* of each of the positions and then to decide which set of consequences it is that you prefer to come about.

1. Teaching race relations may be necessary in a class that has children of more than one race in it. But in one-group classes there are no problems of intergroup or race relations, and there is no point in raising the matter.

2. Much of the hostility and violence in our society today is the result of so much discussion about race. There was a time a few

years ago when things were quiet and peaceful. People did not say at every opportunity that they disliked or even hated other races. In classrooms, we ought to emphasize kindness and politeness to everyone and stop all this talk about race.

3. Many teachers are just not qualified to discuss matters of race relations. They do not know the facts about race; they do not know how to deal with children who are discussing such things and may get excited and upset. Such teachers would do more harm than good in adding the subject to their curriculum. They ought to just teach what they are qualified to teach.

4. All children have been affected—one way or another—by life in a racist society. They have fears, hatreds, misconceptions. Their self-concepts are unrealistic. Many are hopelessly discouraged by the time they reach the fourth grade. Many more are hopelessly circumscribed by that time. If the teacher is to produce children who can act effectively to develop and maintain a democratic society, she must help them understand the reality and develop skills for coping with it. If the teacher is to address herself to the needs of the child, she must see that children need help in problems arising out of racism. If she does not feel qualified to do these things, she must take steps to become qualified or she must give up teaching.

5. Teachers cannot take it on themselves to teach about race relations when parents and school administratoes do not want the subject taught. Teachers are supposed to teach according to curricula developed by the experts hired by the school system. It is the Board of Education that decides on the policy of such matters, and the school superintendent who decides what should and should not be taught. It is the job of the teacher to follow their mandates.

ON INTERGROUP EDUCATION: FOR JUNIOR AND SENIOR HIGH SCHOOL STUDENTS (Developed and used by a tenth-grade English teacher)

Choose from the statements below the one that best describes how you feel. Combine them in any way, omit parts that do not apply, and add in your own words whatever might be missing.

The important thing is that at the end you should be able to say about your statement, "This is exactly how I feel."

1. The Blacks today don't realize how good they really have it. None of them are slaves, and a lot of them get government money for just having children. If they keep making a lot of noise and trouble, they're going to be put right back where they started.

2. It's about time that the Negroes got equal rights in America, but the way they've done it has alienated a lot of whites—ones who weren't prejudiced before. I think that if they took it slower it would be better for everyone.

3. Blacks really aren't as bad as some prejudiced people make them out to be. Many Blacks have done a lot for our society. Their natural speed and rhythm has given sports and music fans a lot of entertainment.

4. Prejudice is stupid. Not all Blacks are bad because one or a few or a few thousand happen to be bad, just as all whites or all Orientals can't be judged by what some do. It is the responsibility of each person to prove his own worth to others and to judge the worth of others as individuals.

5. The only way that Blacks, or any other oppressed minority will get any equality is by pushing and stepping on a lot of racist toes. The only way the scales are going to move to a balance is by making them tilt the other way and then swing back. Right on!

ON RACE RELATIONS: FOR FIFTH- AND SIXTH-GRADERS

Below are five points of view about race relations. Pick the point of view that is closest to what you believe, and change the wording until it says exactly what you think. Or you may write a new point of view that is your own. The idea is to be able to get a paragraph about which you can say, "This is my belief."

1. It is better for friends to be of the same race. People of different races don't understand each other and can easily hurt each other's feelings. So it is a good idea for white people to have only white friends and Black people to have only Black friends.

2. People of different races should not attend the same school. Colored people don't do as well in school as white people do, and they keep the class back. It is better for them to be in classes with all colored people, so they can learn as slowly as they need to.

3. Black and white people should work together in school, live in the same neighborhoods and associate socially. There are no real differences between them and there is no reason why they cannot forget about the whole business of different races.

4. Black people in this country have been badly hurt by white people. They have been refused jobs, kept out of neighborhoods, given inferior education. It is not easy for Black people to just forget about all this and be friends with white people. It is better for Black people to just get what they are entitled to without having anything to do with white people.

5. Black people and white people are all citizens of the same country. They must work together to see to it that everyone has a good job, a good place to live and a good education. If Black people and white people are to work together in this way, they must be friends. Only friends really care for each other, and want to do the best for each other.

ON HAVING BLACK NEIGHBORS: FOR INTERMEDIATE PUPILS (Developed and used by a fourth-grade teacher)

You have just learned that your new neighbors are Black. Pick the statement below that expresses your own feeling.

1. You feel upset. You can't understand why this situation had to happen to you.

2. You feel happy. You are interested in learning more about a race you have little knowledge of.

3. You are not sure how you feel. You would like to accept your new neighbors but you have heard too many bad things about their race.

4. You feel that your neighborhood will start to decline. You are fearful of crime and gang warfare.

ON RACE RELATIONS: FOR FIRST GRADERS
(Developed and used by a first-grade teacher)

Listen to the stories I am going to tell you and look at the pictures to help you remember what I said. Put a circle around the picture which best tells how you feel.

1. Learning about Black people and Puerto Rican people is fun. I like to be in a class with Black people and Puerto Rican people. They should be friends and play together.

2. I don't like to talk about Black people and Puerto Rican people. Black children should play with Black children and Puerto Rican children should play with Puerto Rican children.

3. Black people are better than Puerto Rican people. Some Puerto Rican people are all right to play with.

4. Puerto Rican people are better than Black people. Some Black people are all right to play with.

ON SCHOOL INTEGRATION: FOR TEACHERS AND PROSPECTIVE TEACHERS (Developed and used by a supervisor in a staff development program for teachers)

Below are four points of view about race relations. Pick the point of view that is closest to what you believe and change the wording until it says exactly what you think. Or you may write a new point of view that is your own. The idea is to be able to get a paragraph about which you can say, "This is my belief."

1. White and Black children should go to separate schools. White children will learn more when they are with all white children and Black children will learn more in a school composed of all Black children. Once in a while, the groups can be mixed for special district events.

2. Black children should be bussed into all white schools because they will learn more in an integrated environment. During all school activities, white and Black students should be grouped together. Time should be spent before school and during lunch for playing together.

3. White and Black children should go to the same schools, but should be placed into separate classes. This will prevent the white children from picking up poor discipline habits from the Black children. The white children will also be able to move more quickly in their learning, and will not frustrate the Black children in their inability to keep up.

4. Black and white children should attend the same schools because only in this integrated environment will real learning in life take place. Black children will be able to give the white children a deeper feeling of reality about life. They will help the white children learn to live in a world of many races of people and will in turn learn the same from the white children.

A VALUE SHEET WITH A TWIST: FOR INTERMEDIATE CHILDREN (Developed and used by a language arts teacher)

Our Alphabet

a	b	c	d	e	f	g	h	i	j	k	l	m	n	o	p	q	r	s	t	u	v	w	x	y
z	y	x	w	v	u	t	s	r	q	p	o	n	m	l	k	j	i	h	g	f	e	d	c	b

Code

Use this code to translate the following statements. Then pick the statement that expresses your own point of view.

1. Zoo prmwh lu kvlkov hslfow olev lmv zmlgsvi.
2. Kvlkov tlggz yv uivv.
3. Ylim uivv.
4. Dszg gsv dliow mvvwh mld rh olev.
5. Hzev gsv xlfmgib.
6. Z xszmtv rh tlmmz xlnv.
7. Vfvibylwb'h yvzfgrufo.
8. Dv hszoo levixlnv.

ON DRUG USE: FOR HIGH SCHOOL STUDENTS

Below are five points of view about drug use. Pick the point of view that is closest to what you believe, and change the wording until it says exactly what you think. Or you may write a new point of view that is your own. The idea is to be able to get a paragraph about which you can say, "This is my belief."

1. I don't know what all the fuss is about drugs. People have been smoking marijuana for years with no bad effects. And heroin and speed don't hurt you if you don't overdo it. Anyway, anyone with will-power can stop whenever he wants to.

2. Using drugs is stupid. A person shouldn't even take aspirin without a doctor's advice, because aspirin can be harmful too, and even addicting.

3. Marijuana is all right to use in moderation—like smoking cigarettes or drinking alcoholic beverages. Having laws against marijuana is like prohibition, and apparently most people didn't want that very much.

4. Drugs like marijuana, heroin, barbiturates and alcohol apparently give users temporary feelings of well-being. It would make more sense if we could work to make living satisfying in fact, so that we wouldn't need to delude ourselves with drugs.

ON SEXUAL RELATIONS: FOR ELEMENTARY STUDENTS

Below are four points of view about boy-girl relations. Pick the point of view that is closest to what you believe, and change the wording until it says exactly what you think. Or you may write a new point of view that is your own. The idea is to be able to get a paragraph about which you can say, "This is my belief."

1. It is better for boys and girls to go to separate schools. They don't get along well together and they just keep each other from doing well in school.

2. Boys and girls should go to the same schools but they ought to have separate classes. This way, teachers can teach boys what they ought to know and girls what they ought to know, because in life they need to know different things.

3. Boys and girls should go to school together and be in the same classes. It is important for them to learn to work together and enjoy each other's company so that when they are grown up they can get along well and be happy with each other.

4. There are some things that boys need to learn and some that girls need to learn. Therefore, it is better to teach them some things in separate classes. For everything else, they can be in class together, even though they sometimes pick on each other and get into arguments.

ON SEXUAL RELATIONS: FOR HIGH SCHOOL STUDENTS

Below are five points of view about sexual relations. Pick the point of view that is closest to what you believe, and change the wording until it says exactly what you think. Or you may write a new point of view that is your own. The idea is to be able to get a paragraph about which you can say, "This is my belief."

1. It is immoral to have sexual intercourse before marriage. No argument can change the fact that this kind of immorality causes all kinds of personal unhappiness. And if it continues unchecked it will cause the destruction of civilization as we know it.

2. It is a good idea to find out if you have any sexual problems before you get married. If you have some sexual experiences before marriage—including sexual intercourse—you have a better chance of having a successful marriage later on.

3. If you love someone, one way to show your love is by engaging in sexual intercourse. This is as natural as holding hands and should not be thought of as bad or immoral.

4. Holding hands, kissing and petting is all right if you love each other. But sexual intercourse before marriage is out. To kiss and pet with someone you don't love is as immoral as intercourse before marriage.

5. All sexual activity, from kissing to intercourse, is as necessary as eating, and there should be no talk of morality in connection with it.

ON SCHOOL INTEGRATION: FOR WHITE HIGH SCHOOL STUDENTS IN AREAS WHERE INDIANS LIVE

Below are 5 points of view about Indian people. Pick the point of view that is closest to what you believe, and change the wording until it says exactly what you think. Or you may write a new point of view that is your own. The idea is to be able to get a paragraph about which you can say, "This is my belief".

1. The Indian people are colorful and interesting, with a history and a way of doing things that are different. Indian festivals and parades where they wear traditional dress and do ancient dances are fun and exciting. Outsiders just don't understand our feeling for the Indians.

2. Indians are lazy and don't take advantage of the opportunities in this country. They think that just because they were here first the world owes them something. After all, they *did* lose the battles with the Americans, so why should they get special treatment?

3. Indian people are just like Black people, Chicanos, Puerto Ricans and other minority groups in their struggle against prejudice and discrimination. They are entitled to equality of opportunity and a fair share of our country's resources, and they have a right to demand what is their due.

4. The Indians were robbed of their land and then systematically murdered almost to extinction. They are entitled to full repayment for everything that was done to them, and if the government won't pay up, they should seize what is rightfully theirs.

5. There is no future in the United States for the Indian people. The only way they can make a decent life for themselves is in complete separation from the domination and exploitation of whites. Whether this is done in separate communities or in a separate country is something for the Indian people to decide, just as they should be free to decide about everything that concerns them.

Making a Change: Simulation

Without smiling, efficiently and almost grimly, I distributed the following forms, one to each pupil in the class.

OATH OF LOYALTY
Durrey School

I, _____, (Print Name—including middle initial) do hereby certify that I will not engage in any way in an attempt to disrupt and/or destroy the school or this class by force, violence or misbehavior.

I further certify that I understand the aforegoing statement is made subject to the penalties of perjury, which here is punishable by an F for the course and expulsion from school.

Signed _____

Then I said, "Before we take up the subject of drugs, I am asking you to sign this sheet. When you've all signed it and returned it to me, we can officially begin." Then I barricaded myself behind my desk and waited.

I looked around at the faces bent over the forms, and saw growing puzzlement, disbelief, shock and anger gradually appear. Several people were merely signing the form, with no indication that they were being asked to do anything out of the ordinary. Others began to ask questions:

"Is this a school policy?"

"No," I answered, "It's for this class only."

"Do you have the power to expel someone from the school?"

"Maybe not directly. But I assure you that I would use my influence to get you out if you violated the oath."

"I can't believe it! Why are you doing this?"

I came out from behind my desk and stood in front of the class.

"You know very well why I'm doing this! You know what's going on in high schools these days! I just want to protect myself. I don't want anyone trying to break up this class!"

One girl, her voice trembling with trepidation and anger, forced the words between stiff jaws, "What gives you the right to make us sign this?"

"I'm the instructor of this course and what I say here goes. If you don't like it, *you* go."

She began to gather her things together, ready to leave.

"My advisor never said anything about this sort of thing when he recommended the class. I'm just going to go and talk to him."

I raised my voice, "You walk out of here and that's it!" There was a strained silence, and then one young man spoke tentatively, "I thought I knew you from last term. I'm so disappointed."

"Disappointed, hell. It's a matter of survival. I know you kids have some weird ideas about drug use, and I'm not going to permit any interference with my teaching. I've got a job to do, and I'm going to do it."

One student got up and handed me the form. "Oh, here. I signed it." She thrust it at me.

Another student did the same: "Me, too."

A third student ostentatiously tore his up with a great show of contempt.

A fourth student handed me the form. I looked at it and then at him. "This isn't signed," I said.

"That's right."

"Aren't you going to sign it?"

"No."

"Well—we can't start this class. Just what do you intend to do?"

I looked around at the class again and saw anger, frustration, tears in one girl's eyes. I couldn't keep up the pretense, and my tone changed.

"What," I said, "can students do when faced with such a situation?"

Suddenly, there were smiles of relief on all the faces. One student pounded his desk and snorted with disgust that he was taken in. Another said, "I knew you couldn't mean it. It was so out of character!"

"Well, suppose you make some plans about what to do if you were really confronted with such a requirement."

Students were then given a choice of follow-up activities designed to help them deal realistically with such an unacceptable regulation. One group decided to develop a plan of action for challenging the loyalty oath, defining step by step the available sources for redress, from trying to convince the teacher that she was wrong to boycotting the class. They then proceeded to take each step, role-playing the action and then replaying to achieve a more desirable goal.

For example, the group asked for an appointment with the instructor to present arguments for abandoning the loyalty oath. The instructor was cold and adamant at this "challenge to her authority." One student became increasingly hostile at the teacher's behavior, made several sarcastic remarks, and with a final "Heil Hitler," stomped out of the room. The teacher announced that the interview was at an end, and the other students withdrew to redefine their strategy. The first thing they did was to point out to the hostile student that his behavior had solidified the teacher's position rather than encouraged her to reconsider. He insisted that nothing would move her. One of the others disagreed, maintaining that a conciliatory manner and logical arguments would be more likely to reach an instructor who was both fearful of loss of authority and also intelligent, well-informed, and eminently qualified in her field.

The angry student said that he could never maintain a conciliatory attitude in the face of stubborness. The others prevailed upon him, then, merely to listen in the background while one or two of them did all the talking. He felt that he could manage that, and they requested another appointment.

Throughout the gathering of information and the testing of different plans, students were encouraged 1) to stop and talk about what they were learning about themselves and others, 2) to express their feelings freely, 3) to clarify issues for themselves and 4) to take stands on issues. One way or another everyone was involved in role-playing the actions taken.

When it was all over, the students felt that they had learned much about how to effect change, and they felt more comfortable about their ability to participate productively in the change process.

Making a Change in the Classroom

The teacher may feel that the following procedure is extremely risky, entailing as it does permitting students to decide how they will learn. There is no doubt that with this technique, the teacher must relinquish most of her absolute control over class management. But there is considerable experience, both theoretical and practical, that substantiates the validity of this procedure. In making changes in classroom management, students are developing effective ways of establishing control over their own lives. And we know that students who have a sense of control over their lives and their environment are more likely to succeed in learning in more academic areas.

Psychologically, we know also that people have different styles of learning, and the student forced to learn in an atmosphere that he rejects and in ways not consonant with his style will not learn efficiently—to say nothing of how he will feel about the learning situation.

As far as educational goals are concerned, our profession gives, if nothing else, lip service to the aim of teaching students to be self-initiating, to learn how to learn, to be actively involved in the learning process. My Education students and I have taught even kindergartners to begin to assume responsibility for planning their experiences, with great success. There is no doubt in my mind that students who are lock-stepped through programs are periodically overwhelmed with hostility, restlessness, resentment of faculty and distrust of each other because they are not offered viable choices and a significant measure of freedom of decision. Medical students, Teacher Corpsmen and other groups I have observed all seem to demonstrate such behavior.

To initiate the process of change in the classroom, students may be asked to evaluate the organization of the class they are in, starting with the response to the question: How do you feel about this class? After a general discussion they go on to a more analytical evaluation (perhaps written) based on the following questions:

1. How do you identify the organization of this class: authoritarian, democratic, laissez-faire, other? What specifically has happened that demonstrates your choice?
2. Which mode of organization do you prefer? Try to determine why you prefer it. Has your past experience been largely with this mode? Is there something in your personality that makes this mode most comfortable for you? Have you evidence that this mode is the best for learning?
3. Can you think of specific things to do in this class, using the type of organization you prefer?
4. How do you feel about different members of the class working in the way they prefer? Do you think this would be too confusing? Impossible because the different methods imply different course objectives? Manageable? Justify your point of view.

Special interest in one of the areas brings students together to discuss their analysis and begin to think of alternative modes of organization. One group might examine the various modes of organization, looking at the advantages and disadvantages and the implications of each. Another group might concentrate on specific activities that are within the purview of the subject matter area. A third group, made up of the more introspective students, might want to spend some time sharing their feelings about various learning and organizational styles and trying to determine the implications of those feelings. A fourth group might begin to define broad course objectives, dealing with their own expectations for the course.

After some time, representatives of each group will get together to synthesize the various group suggestions into a plan for running the course. They may consider the idea that it would be better to plan organization and activities for a week or a month (depending on the age of the group) and then to evaluate their success before planning for a longer period. They would, perhaps, prefer to plan for the achievement of a single objective before going on to a second and third objective.

It should be remembered that the teacher is a part of the discussion and planning at every level. As long as she does not reserve for herself the role of final arbiter, she does have a function that includes the raising of pertinent questions, the offering of information, the suggesting of other resources, and all the other things that teachers know how to do.

The final plan is then submitted to the whole class for ratification. Thus, from beginning to end of this process, the students are 1) making choices, 2) practicing critical thinking, 3) practicing short- and long-term planning, 4) dealing with interpersonal and intergroup relations and 5) committing themselves to responsibility. Meanwhile, the teacher is diagnosing additional educational needs of her students and planning for ways to fill them.

Making a Change in the School

In one elementary school, the Student Council was a rubber-stamp operation, limited in its function to approving what the teachers and administration advanced as policy. Even with this limitation, there were still broadly defined areas where they were not even permitted to express a public point of view.

Some time ago, the school board brought up the question of sex education. Some vocal members of the community were absolutely against the introduction of the subject into the curriculum. Most of the teachers were saying nothing about it at all. Nobody had asked the pupils to express an opinion.

A group of sixth-graders, during a social studies discussion, expressed some feelings about the controversy and wondered aloud about the role of the students in it. They wondered what would happen if they tried to raise the subject at the next Student Council meeting.

The teacher encouraged them to role-play some interaction—

with their representatives, with the elected officers, with the faculty advisor of the Council and even with the principal. Out of this they developed a number of strategies for dealing with the anticipated responses to their request for an airing of the issue, and eventually succeeded in getting it on the Council's agenda.

In their experiences in the community (see Chapter 7), they had met many adults with whom they felt free to raise the question of sex education. They discovered that the vocal community group taking a stand against it was by no means representative of the adults in the community. So, they took the initiative and invited some of their community friends to express their point of view at a Council meeting.

Along the way, they began to examine all the points of view and clarify for themselves just where they stood on the issue. They also encouraged their schoolmates in other classes to do the same. Two of the pupils even prevailed upon a friendly fifth-grade teacher to permit them to do a problem census in one of her classes. Asking the question: "What do you want to know about sex?" got a serious listing of concerns that moved the teacher to speak at a parent-teacher meeting on behalf of those concerns.

At one point, some of the sixth-graders insisted that if they did not get in school what they felt they were entitled to in the way of sex education, they would organize a "Free School" and ask for volunteer instructors from the community to teach them.

The issue has not yet been resolved. However, the activity alone —the talking, the planning, the openness, the trying out of various strategies—has been an education for everyone involved. Even before it is ever included in the curriculum, sex education has become a part of the experience of the school and the community. Most importantly, the children are learning what it means to become involved in social change. They are feeling that sense of power and control over their own lives that helps them see themselves as worthwhile people with viable goals. And this is as good a definition of the mentally-healthy citizen of a democracy as any I have ever heard.

The Last Word

Occasionally, when my course on these strategies is almost over, a teacher will come to me with "a problem." She has a difficult class, she tells me. She is sure they have all kinds of group prejudices or problems about drugs, but she does not know what to do with them —how to start or where it will lead her. I always ask, "Have you done a problem census with them?" "Well, no—not with that group," she says. "I've done it with my other classes, but not with them. *I don't know what answers I'll get if I try it.*"

Therein lies the key to the problem! The teacher is so afraid to find out what the kids think, that she has avoided the obvious place to start. Ask the first question: What do you want to know about race? (or about drugs, or sex). Then begin to teach to the responses —whatever they are. *That is where you start.* As you go along, you provide all the experiences with race or drugs or sex that you can, using all the techniques you have learned. Gradually, the children and the teacher become more comfortable in talking about the topic. Little by little they add to their store of information. Slowly and painfully they begin to explore solutions to problems. And then one day they begin to take an active part in solving those problems.

Above all, we cannot reserve these experiences for selected students, or older students. I remember one teacher who insisted that "Feelings are abstract. That's why you have to wait until students are mature and are able to deal with feelings." The sad fact was that she did not even recognize feelings when she heard them expressed! She listened to an affective discussion in a second grade and heard a comment by a Black child: "When white people go by, they smile at the children but they don't like the grown-ups." She listened to this child and to other similar expressions and then concluded that the children were too young to express their feelings! So she discontinued the discussion and went back to "teaching" them.

What a sad note on which to end the book!